From
TEE TO GREEN

From TEE TO GREEN

Bill Robertson
Illustrations by Graham Gaches

Bramley Books

3039
© 1993 CLB Publishing Ltd., Godalming, Surrey
This edition published 1993 by Bramley Books
Printed and bound in Italy by New Interlitho SPA, Milan
ISBN 1 85833 033 5

Contents

Introduction

Having played golf for over twenty years I've experienced all the common problems of the game and hooked, sliced, pushed, pulled, topped and shanked my way around some of the finest courses in the world. I've also thrown clubs in frustration, sworn to give the game up and missed more three foot putts than I would like to remember.

However, I have also been fortunate enough to play with many top professionals and work with some of the most gifted teaching professionals in the game. One or two have looked at my swing and then suggested that I take up another sport, but thankfully the vast majority have been sympathetic enough to pass on numerous hints and tips, in an effort to help cure whatever ill was currently plaguing my game.

If you can hit a high draw with a 1 iron from a bare lie, stop a 3 iron dead in its tracks, and more often than not, get up and down in two from a greenside bunker, then this book is not for you. If on the other hand you miss more fairways than you hit, struggle with the long irons, dread bunker shots but still can't wait to get out on the golf course each weekend, then you might just find some encouragement within the pages of this book.

Bill Robertson

CHAPTER ONE

From the tee

The fade and the draw

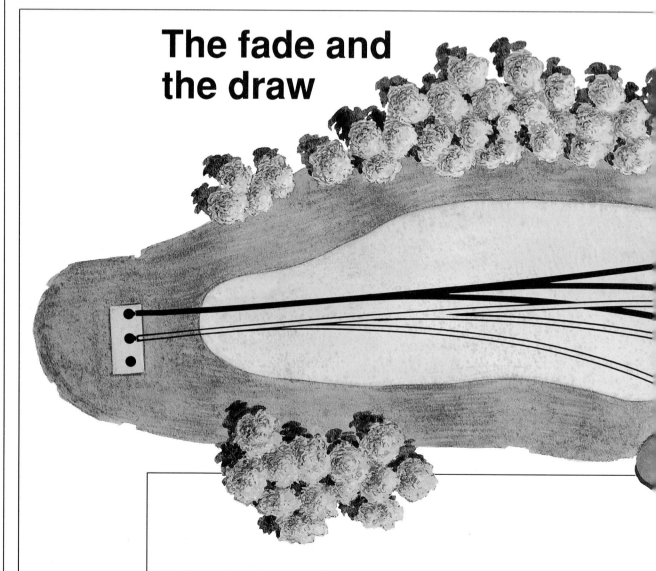

V ery few golfers, including the top professionals, hit the ball dead straight, especially with the driver. From the tee, the better players tend to draw the ball, while the majority of the higher handicappers usually hit a fade. You should always be aware of your natural shot, be it fade or draw, when it comes to teeing-up, especially if there is trouble on either side of the fairway.

For example, in the hole illustrated, there is double trouble, with trees down the left of the hole and water, in the form of a lake, severely guarding the right side of the fairway.

Let us suppose that you normally fade the ball with the driver. In that case, you should always tee-up as close as you can to the left side of the tee. Then aim your drive down the left side of the fairway. If everything goes to plan, your natural fade will turn the ball right into the centre of the fairway. If you hit a straight shot, the ball will still end up in the fairway. And if the worst happens and that fade becomes a slice, then because you have started the

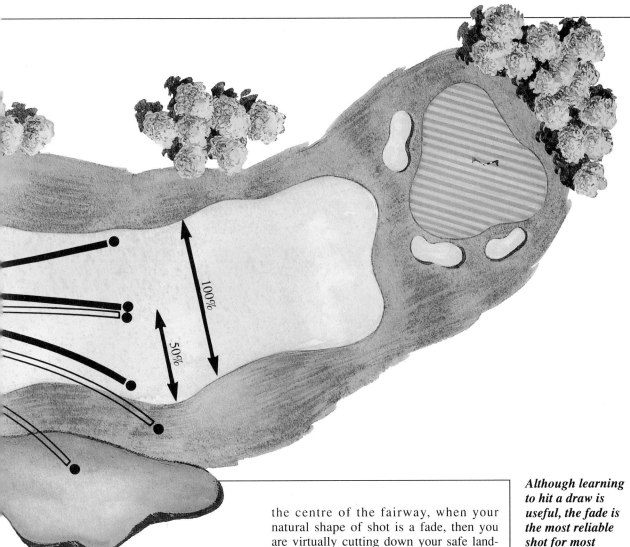

100%

50%

Although learning to hit a draw is useful, the fade is the most reliable shot for most players.

the centre of the fairway, when your natural shape of shot is a fade, then you are virtually cutting down your safe landing area by up to fifty per cent.

When preparing to hit your tee shot, try to find a level area. Remember, you can tee the ball up as far back as two club lengths from the line between the two tee markers. Some amateur golfers feel that unless they can draw the ball they will never become better players. Certainly there are advantages to be gained from being able to hit the right to left shot, especially when it comes to distance. However, when it comes to accuracy, the fade is by far the most reliable shot and the one favoured by many of the top players, including Nicklaus and Ballesteros.

shot down the left side of the hole, chances are the ball will still hold the right side of the fairway, or stop in the semi-rough.

If on the other hand, you were set up in the centre of the teeing arc and follow the same sequence of shot pattern, the results would be as follows. A straight shot will finish in the centre of the fairway, a fade will carry the ball into the right-hand rough and a slice will end up in the lake!

By allowing for your percentage shot, you can use the whole width of the fairway. However, if you choose to play for

Judging your distances

Although we weekend golfers may not be able to hit the ball as far as the Greg Normans and Seve Ballesteros' of this world, it is just as important for us to know how far we hit the ball as it is for the top stars.

Personally speaking, I probably miss as many greens through hitting the wrong club, as I do by playing the wrong shot. And the reason that I hit the wrong club is because I usually have no idea how far I have actually hit the ball from the tee, and subsequently, how far I still have to go to reach the green.

Some people have a natural feel of distance. Unfortunately I am not one of those fortunate individuals and I have lost count of the number of times I have stood over the ball thinking to myself: "Is it a 6 iron or a 5 or maybe even a 4 iron?" The end result is usually a poor shot because, instead of concentrating on making a good swing, I am still wondering if I have the right club in my hand when I am actually hitting the ball.

Most clubs today have their own yardage chart which I find very helpful when visiting a new course. But I must confess that until recently I have never taken the trouble to work out any specific distances on my own course. A case no doubt of familiarity breeding contempt.

Finally, however, I did take the time to work out a rough distance guide on the par 4 holes. I did this by pacing out approximately 200 yards from the tee on each of the par 4 holes. I looked round for a marker which I could identify easily.

Something such as a bunker, bush or a tree, anything in fact that was easily identifiable to be my 200 yard marker. From that position it was simply a case of subtracting from the overall length of the hole to find out how far I had left to the green.

If you work on the basic premise that there is a 10 yard difference between each club then having a rough 200 yard marker enables you to know approximately how far you are from the green before you play your second shot.

Try the 200 yard marker guide and take the guess work out of your approach shots.

Poor alignment

One of the most common faults among we amateur golfers is poor alignment. And I can think of nothing more frustrating than to hit a tee shot flush off the face of the club, only to find that instead of flying straight down the centre of the fairway, the ball ends up in the rough; not as the result of a hook or a slice, but simply because I failed to take enough care when aiming.

Alignment is a problem that affects golfers at all levels of ability, including the top professionals. However, they are careful enough to keep alignment mistakes to a minimum by adopting a set procedure on almost every shot they hit, which is designed to keep them firmly on the straight and narrow.

There is no secret to this procedure. It is a simple four step system that you too can easily adopt to help eliminate some of those wayward shots.

1. Before you address the ball, stand behind it, look at the hole, or shot you are about to play, and try to picture in your mind the ideal target line. There may be an obvious guide, such as a marker pole or tree in the distance. If not, pick an object or mark on the fairway, a few yards in front of your ball which is on that imaginary target line.

2. Having established the target line, position yourself at right angles to it, placing the clubhead directly behind the ball. Personally, I like to position the club using only my right hand. When I am happy that the face is square to the target line, I then add my left hand to complete the grip. Other golfers prefer to establish

1 Pick out something to aim at on your target line.

2 Place the head of the club behind the ball, square to the target line.

3 Position your body parallel to the intended ball-to-target line.

4 Check that shoulders, hips and feet are all square before starting the backswing.

their grip on the club with both hands before they place the club behind the ball. And as I have seen both methods used by the top pros, I should imagine it is a matter of personal preference, as long as the main objective is to ensure that the clubface is positioned square to the target line.

3. The next step is to position your feet, parallel to the target line, and to help establish the correct ball position, I instigate a little personal drill. First, I stand with my feet together directly opposite the ball. Then I take a half step to the left with my left foot and a full step to the right with my right foot, which has the effect of positioning the ball at a point just inside my left heel at address.

I should add at this point, having set my feet, I sometimes forget to check that my left foot has not crossed the imaginary line which runs parallel to the target line. And the result of my carelessness is often a push to the right or if I'm trying for a big hit from the tee, a vicious pull to the left.

4. The final check is to ensure that both shoulders and hips are parallel to my feet before I start my backswing. The rest I leave to muscle memory and fate!

FROM THE TEE

Making a sensible shoulder turn

If you're the kind of person who, after spending a week behind a desk, can leap from the car, go straight onto the first tee and make a 90 degree shoulder turn while at the same time getting the club into a parallel position before unwinding to send a 300 yard drive down the centre of the fairway, then the following will be of no interest to you whatsoever.

However it is an unfortunate fact of life that many of we amateur golfers find ourselves dashing onto the first tee without having the opportunity or perhaps the inclination, to spend a few minutes loosening up the muscles before playing. Yet undeterred, we step up on the tee, haul out the driver and attempt to emulate the long, supple swing of some athletic young pro we happened to have seen the previous evening, while watching the highlights of a televised tournament.

At best, the outcome is usually a poor tee shot: at worst, a pulled muscle.

It may be macho, but it certainly is not essential, to achieve a pro-like position at the top of the backswing in order to produce a good shot. Take Sandy Lyle for example; he certainly could not be accused of overswinging, yet he still hits the ball as

far, if not further, than the majority of his fellow professionals.

In a vain effort to get the club back to parallel in the backswing, many amateur golfers destroy what might be a less athletic, but nevertheless sound swing. One common fault which occurs as a result of trying to achieve too big a turn, is allowing the left foot to rise up until only the big toe retains contact with the ground. This can lead to all sorts of swing problems, not to mention the fact that it also destroys the 'winding' effect of the shoulder turn on the upper part of the body; something which is essential, if the downswing is to start correctly.

Forget most of what you see the pros doing on television; they have spent most of their lives hitting golf balls, not to mention at least a couple of hours on the practice ground each day before going out to play their round.

What really matters is making as full a shoulder turn as possible while being able to retain balance and control, without doing yourself an injury in the process. And if by doing so, you are able to turn your left shoulder past the ball in the backswing: so much the better.

(Opposite left) The club has not reached parallel position but I have still managed to make a reasonable shoulder turn whereas (opposite right) I am struggling to get the club past the parallel and am on the way to a hernia!

Topping

For professionals and amateurs alike, the first shot of the day can often determine the outcome of the round. In the case of the tour pro, he at least will have spent time on the practice tee warming up, therefore when it comes to that all important opening drive, the golfing muscles should be loose. The fact that he has probably hit a dozen or so practice drives will also help his chances of making a reasonable swing and finding the fairway with his tee shot.

However, in the case of we weekend golfers, it is more likely to be a matter of arriving at the course about five minutes before we are due to play, dashing to the first tee, taking a few hurried practice swings and then hoping that we get lucky. That is why it is hardly surprising that you see so many opening drives drilled along the ground, instead of through the air.

The only thing that can be said in favour of topping is that the ball usually goes straight. However that is not much of a consolation when you are left with a 250 yard second shot!

The problem with topping is that it is seldom caused by a single fault, rather it is a combination of different errors. One of those faults is the result of tension, both physical and mental. The mental aspect is caused by apprehension about the first shot of the day; where will the ball go and how well will I play today?

This mental tension often transmits itself to the physical side of our game, causing us to grip the club too tightly, setting up tension in the wrists and forearms which in turn inhibits the clubhead from being swung with a natural and free action.

Another major contributor to topping is weight transfer. Keeping the weight too much on the left side during the takeaway can lead to topping the ball, and the same can be said of leaving too much weight on the right side, during the downswing!

FROM TEE TO GREEN

One of the best tips I ever received to avoid topping, especially helpful with regard to that first drive of the round, was not to try to give the ball an almighty thrash. Instead, I was advised to concentrate on playing a three quarter shot with the emphasis on rhythm and balance, rather than distance.

It also helps if you take your time and do not let yourself be rushed into hitting on the run with a 'let's get this over with as quickly as possible attitude'. By taking your time, you might also avoid another topping trap, that of lifting your head too quickly to look for the ball.

Remember, if you are playing with other golfers, you will have at least one, if not three pairs of eyes to follow the flight of the ball. You should concentrate on watching the ball through impact.

(Opposite) By moving your body through the shot, you will greatly enhance your chances of making a solid contact with the ball.

(Left) Leaving the weight on the right side in the downswing is just one way to top the ball.

Play the percentages

The other week, while playing in a friendly four ball match, we reached the first par 3 hole on the course. Having snaked in a 20 footer from the edge of the green on the previous hole, my partner had the honour and I was surprised to see him drop the ball onto the turf instead of using a tee peg. Granted, it was a fairly short hole, measuring just over 120 yards, and the fact that he had not teed the ball up did not appear to inhibit his shot. In fact the ball looked to be flying right at the flag but when it landed, instead of stopping quickly, it took a big bounce and ran some 20 feet past the hole.

As we walked towards the green, I asked my partner why he did not use a tee peg. He replied that he liked to hit down on the ball with his lofted clubs and when he played from a tee, he felt that he had to change his swing and attempt to lift the ball up in the air. Usually it made no difference to the flight of the shot but he did confess that he often found that the ball tended to run on when it landed on the green, even with a lofted club such as the 8 iron he had just played.

As we approached the green my partner mentioned that the part of the top pro's

When grass gets between the ball and clubface, it can lead to loss of control on a good swing producing a bad shot.

18

FROM TEE TO GREEN

game which impressed him the most was the way in which they were able to stop the ball quickly and, in some instances, make it spin back towards the hole, especially with the short irons. It was then that I suggested that the next time he had the opportunity to watch the top men in action, he should count the number of times he notices anyone not using a tee peg on a par three hole. And I then bet him a fiver that he could count the instances on the fingers of one hand.

The reason I was so confident about winning my bet stems from the fact that professional golfers are always seeking the best possible lie from which to play a shot. Practice has given them a high degree of control over how far they hit the ball and the shape of flight they wish to achieve,

but a less than perfect lie can add an element of chance to a shot and therefore they are not fully in charge of the outcome of the shot.

However, when it comes to hitting from the tee, the pros take full advantage of being able to give themselves the best possible lie from which to play their shot. And when it comes to par three holes, the fact that they can tee the ball up ensures that they don't have to contend with the grass getting between the back of the ball and the clubface at impact. When this happens, as it frequently does when playing from the semi rough or very lush fairways, the amount of backspin can be greatly reduced, causing the ball to run further when it lands, instead of sitting down quickly by the hole.

Any time you get the opportunity to improve your lie, take it. You will make cleaner contact with the ball when it is teed-up and improve your chances of a better result.

Position not distance

The next time you stand on the tee at a long or difficult par 4 hole, instead of pulling out your driver and hoping for the best, why not try a different approach? Instead of looking from the tee to the distant green, pick a target area on the fairway which you feel confident of reaching with your tee shot. It might be a good idea, especially if your handicap allows you a shot at the hole, to hit a 3 wood instead of the driver; play for position, not distance.

Having reached your first objective, repeat the process with your second shot resisting the temptation to play a long iron, or fairway wood in the hope of reaching the green. Pick instead, another target area, short of the putting surface and comfortably within range with a medium iron. Try to choose a target area, even if it is still well short of the green, which leaves a straightforward third shot to the flag.

A less than perfect pitch shot, should still reach the green and two putts will give you a net par at a difficult hole. However, a well played approach shot could put you within single putt distance of the hole and the reward for three sensible shots and a good putt, could be a net birdie.

A few moments' careful consideration of how to play a difficult par 4 will pay dividends.

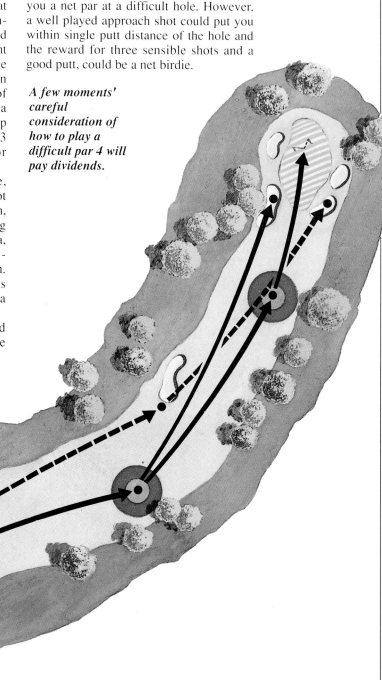

CHAPTER TWO

The swing

Hitting through not at the ball

Hitting at, instead of swinging through the ball is just one of my many swing faults. Although I try to swing slowly and smoothly with the shorter irons, I often succumb to the temptation to whack the ball with the woods and long irons.

Hitting hard at the ball normally leads to almost a stabbing action instead of the correct, smooth build up of power. This type of action can also lead to hitting down on the ball and skying or even smothering the shot.

Another tip to help overcome this problem is to imagine that there are two golf balls: one real, one imaginary. In order to produce a good shot it is necessary to swing through the first ball, and on to impact with the imaginary second ball which is positioned about six inches in front of the actual ball.

This is not very easy to do immediately and it will help if you spend a few minutes on the practice ground, using two tee pegs as substitutes for golf balls getting the feel of swinging through to the second tee peg.

By concentrating on swinging through to the imaginary ball you will avoid stabbing at the real ball and hopefully produce a better contact.

To help promote a feeling of swinging through the shot, imagine you are trying to make contact with a second ball, six inches in front of your actual ball.

The downswing drill

Aproblem which often troubles golfers like myself who are all too often preoccupied with hitting at the ball instead of swinging the club through the ball, is failing to clear the left side properly in the downswing.

Because I am concentrating on hitting the ball hard, my downswing begins with a rush which normally leads to the right shoulder coming over the top. This leads to the club travelling on an out-to-in path which causes a slice if I leave the clubface open at impact, or in the case of a short iron, a pull to the left if I manage to square the face of the club through impact.

Of all the various components in the golf swing, the start of the downswing is perhaps the most critical area. You may have a perfect grip, superb posture, a slow, smooth takeaway and a wonderful shoulder turn. But, if you do not start the downswing properly, chances are the result will be a poor shot.

There are several theories on how to start the downswing. However, the one that has worked the best for me is as you start your downswing, to try to imagine that someone who is standing behind you, has taken hold of your left trouser pocket and that they are pulling your left hip back as the club swings down towards the ball.

Keeping this image in my mind has helped in two ways. Firstly, it focuses the mind on the lower part of the body at the start of the downswing and by doing so, helps prevent the upper body in the shape of the right shoulder, becoming too dominant.

Secondly, the thought of the hand pulling at my left hand trouser pocket, helps me concentrate on clearing my left side properly in the downswing which in turn, allows the club to swing along the correct in-to-out swing path.

Although this has helped me to overcome right shoulder dominance in the downswing, it takes a little time and practice to achieve the correct timing and co-ordination. At the start, I still had a tendency to rush things and this led to my hips spinning too quickly to the left instead of clearing smoothly and allowing my hands and arms to swing the club through at a controlled pace.

However, with a little effort and patience you might find this exercise will help to cure one of the most annoying swing faults in the game.

Imagine a hand pulling your left trouser pocket backwards to help clear your hips properly in the downswing.

Turn, don't tilt

Overswing can often be more harmful than swinging short. When the club travels well beyond the horizontal, it can lead to several problems including chopping down on the ball, poor balance and lack of proper weight transfer, to name but a few.

Unfortunately, it is extremely difficult to gauge the length of your backswing other than by watching yourself in a mirror at home. Some golfers, especially the younger ones, are fit and supple and find it comparatively easy to swing the club back beyond the horizontal. Others who are perhaps not as supple as they once were still contrive to get the club wrapped round their neck.

Most middle aged golfers fool themselves into believing that they are still making a good, full shoulder turn when what they are actually doing is tilting rather than turning. And it is a fact that we can also find it easier to get the club further round by using a narrow stance and letting the left heel come well up off the ground in the backswing.

Now there is nothing wrong with letting the left heel rise up but when this combines with too narrow a stance and a tilting shoulder action, then it is usually a recipe for disaster.

Another problem caused by a narrow stance, especially with the longer clubs like the driver, is that it encourages the hips to turn too much and too soon in the backswing which, although it helps get the club round, fails to encourage the proper winding, or coiling action.

This coiling action is one of the keys to both power and timing because by restricting the amount of hip turn in the backswing you can physically feel the muscles being wound. And it is the controlled release of those big muscles in the legs and left side which help produce much of the power in the golf swing.

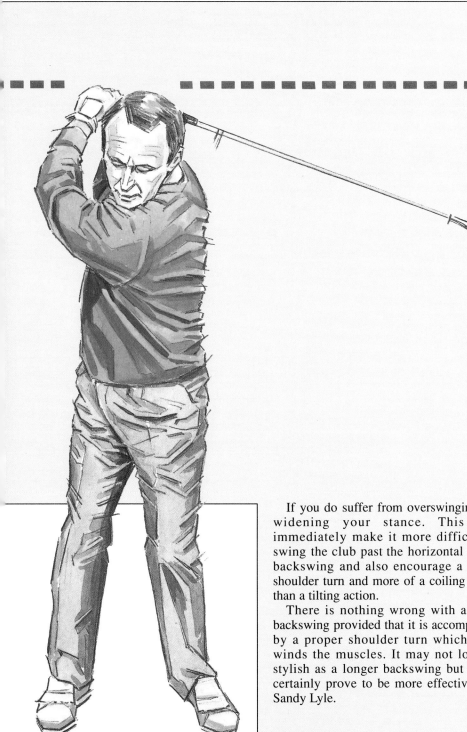

If you do suffer from overswinging, try widening your stance. This will immediately make it more difficult to swing the club past the horizontal in the backswing and also encourage a better shoulder turn and more of a coiling rather than a tilting action.

There is nothing wrong with a short backswing provided that it is accompanied by a proper shoulder turn which fully winds the muscles. It may not look as stylish as a longer backswing but it can certainly prove to be more effective; ask Sandy Lyle.

(Opposite left) Wider stance promotes good coiling action in the backswing. (Left) Too narrow a stance encourages overswing and a tendency to dip, instead of turn.

Time for a change

One of the main reasons most handicap golfers slice their shots is that they tend to swing the club on an out-to-in swing path. This is normally the result of the right shoulder coming over the top in the downswing and causing the clubface to cut across the ball at impact.

If you suffer from this problem, try imagining that at the address position, the ball is resting in the centre of a clock face.

When you slice the ball, the clubhead will have been travelling from between two o'clock and three, to a position between eight o'clock and nine.

Before you start your backswing, this time, try to imagine the clubface travelling across the clockface from a position between three and four o'clock, through the ball and on to a point between nine and ten o'clock.

Use the image of a clock face to help beat the slice.

Think swing — not hit

One of the most obvious differences between a top professional and the weekend golfer is rhythm. While we amateurs all too frequently tend to lunge at the ball, certainly when it comes to the woods and long irons, the pros just seem to swing the club at the same pace, regardless of the club they are using.

Unfortunately, as with most things in a golf swing, there is no magical formula for success and almost without exception, those smooth and rhythmical swings are the result of many years of hard work on the practice ground. However, although we may never be as good strikers of the ball as the pros, there is no reason why we cannot try to think like them, especially when it comes to the subject of rhythm and timing.

I once asked a well-known tournament professional what he thinks about when he is hitting the ball. "Nothing at all" was the rather caustic reply. But when I pressed him a little further he revealed that unless he was working on a specific part of his swing, such as his take-away, or shoulder turn, he tried to keep his mind clear of any of the technical aspects of the swing.

He continued, "I have hit so many practice balls that my swing now works almost completely from muscle memory and I try not to interfere with that process too much when I'm on the course playing a competitive round."

However he did say that from time to time he had problems with his driving when his timing went off and his rhythm became a little too quick.

He said, "When I stand on the tee, although I have the driver in my hand, I try to imagine that it is a 7 iron. As I never try to hit a 7 iron hard, this helps me to concentrate on rhythm and not distance with the result that I sometimes actually hit the ball further than normal."

(Right) To help encourage a smooth rhythm when using woods or long irons, try to imagine that you are swinging a 7 iron.

Extension

Some golfers tend to cut their swing off short after impact, believing that once the clubhead has struck the ball, there is nothing further they can do to influence the flight of the ball or the outcome of the shot.

Unfortunately this philosophy couldn't be further from the truth. The golfers who tend to chop at the ball, rather than swing through it with little or no follow-through, are in fact quitting on the shot and therefore failing to generate anything like their full power at impact.

In a good swing, the thought should be to try to feel that the club is still accelerating *after* it strikes the ball, and that the

(Opposite) Quitting on the shot.

(Above) Accelerating the club after it strikes the ball.

natural forces generated by transferring the body weight through the shot actually pull the hands and arms through the shot and on to a full follow through.

This principle applies regardless of the length of the backswing. Sandy Lyle has a comparatively short backswing but produces a full and beautifully balanced follow through with every full shot.

The only time you see a top professional shortening his follow through is when playing a punch shot or when his ball is plugged in a bunker or buried in heavy rough, or alternatively when he is hitting a three-quarter, or short shot.

Another benefit which comes from accelerating the club through the shots comes from the way that the arms are then extended along the target line. This is something that helps keep the clubhead travelling towards the target a little longer to produce a more accurate shot. One man who does this superbly is Lee Trevino.

However, be careful not to over emphasize the extension of the arms through the shot because you could end up doing yourself an injury. Better to work on the idea of the club being pulled down the target line through impact before the natural turn of the left side fully clears the hips and pulls the arms around and up into a full and well balanced finish.

Pace pointer

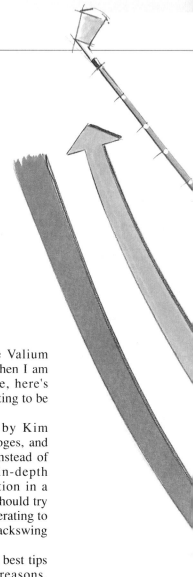

I have always thought that one of the main reasons why golf is such a difficult game to master is the fact that many of the important functions of the swing take place behind you, where it is impossible to see what is going on.

Am I taking the club back too much on the inside? Is the club pointing at the target when it reaches the top of the backswing? Is my left wrist arched or cupped just before I start the club down?

To be honest, more times than not I haven't a clue because I'm trying to keep my eyes firmly fixed on the ball!

At the end of the day it is more a case of trusting my instincts and hoping for the best which, as most weekend golfers like myself will appreciate, is hardly a technique which breeds confidence or produces any lasting success.

I am certain that one of the real secrets to hitting consistently good golf shots is the ability to apply sound swing fundamentals without actually thinking about them as you are playing a shot. When I step onto the first tee my mind usually becomes a clutter of swing theories and misconceptions. All too frequently they choose the precise moment when I start my backswing to clamour for prominence in my brain.

I often wish I could instigate some kind of mental 'spring cleaning' exercise that would permit me to wipe the tape blank and start off once again with a simple, uncomplicated mental picture of how to swing the golf club. Sad to say, to date I have failed to achieve that idyllic mental state. However, a recent golf clinic offered a light at the end of the dark tunnel, by providing a simple solution to a potentially complicated question.

"How fast should you swing the club in the downswing?" is just about on a par with "Should you breathe out or in during your backswing?" That is the kind of question that has me fumbling in the

Concentrate on swinging twice as fast on the downswing as you did on the backswing to help the pace of your swing.

bottom of my golf bag for the Valium tablets. Terrific, I thought, just when I am up to my eyeballs in technique, here's another mental minefield just waiting to be set off.

The golf clinic was given by Kim Thomas, professional at Stoke Poges, and it gave me a pleasant surprise. Instead of launching into an hour long in-depth analysis he answered the question in a single sentence by saying: "You should try to think of your downswing accelerating to about twice the speed of your backswing as you strike the ball."

This is one of the simplest and best tips I have ever received, for two reasons. Firstly, in the downswing it provides a gauge for regulating the speed of an action which previously had been haphazard, because in my case it had never before been linked to the pace of my backswing.

The second benefit to come from Kim's simple statement was that it encouraged me to make a slow, smooth backswing. Only by taking the club back slowly was I able to create any feel for the pace I should be aiming to achieve in my downswing.

It took a whole practice session to put Kim's advice into operation but it was well worth the effort. It gave me a simple swing thought which I could use without tying myself up with too much swing theory.

Three steps to better ball position

Step One

F inding the correct ball position in your stance can sometimes prove to be a complicated exercise. Some top teachers feel that the ball position should remain constant at just inside the left heel whatever the club; other equally respected professionals maintain that it should move to the right, as you progress through the driver to the wedge. In the end, it usually comes down to the individual experimenting to find out what system produced the best results for them.

However, when it comes to establishing how far you should stand from the ball at the address position, there is a simple but reliable method of determining the correct distance, and one which works for everyone, be they tall, short, fat, thin, old or young.

Start by standing with both feet together, gripping the club in the normal manner. Then, extend it away from you until it is at arms' length and horizontal to the ground.

The next move is to bend forward from the waist, while keeping the legs straight, until the sole of the club touches the ground. At this point, spread your feet to take up your normal width of stance, at the same time allowing your knees to flex slightly. You will find that this system works not just for the driver, as illustrated above, but also for all the other clubs in the bag.

Now if you find that you are getting some strange looks trying this tip out on the course, you can practise it in the privacy of your own home until the correct ball position becomes second nature.

Step Two

Step Three

Pull the handle

It is generally accepted, that although there may be a variety of ways to take the club back from the ball, there is only one way to return it correctly, and that is on a slight in-to-out swing path.

Seve Ballesteros picks the club up steeply outside the line in the backswing; Jack Nicklaus is famous for his flying right elbow; and Lee Trevino looks odds on to hit the ball straight left as the result of his takeaway. But one thing all these great players have in common is that they come back to the ball from inside the target line.

One of the major differences between the top players and we amateurs, is that from the top of the backswing, they are thinking 'swing through' and we are thinking 'hit at'. The outcome in our case is usually the right shoulder coming over the top, leaving the clubhead travelling along an out-to-in swing path, and inevitably resulting in a sliced shot.

There are many different methods of trying to restrain this destructive right shoulder action. Believe me I have tried most of them. But one that has provided more help than most, is trying to concentrate on pulling the butt, or end, of the handle of the club, down towards the ball in the downswing.

For me, this action has two advantages. Firstly it makes my left arm more conscious, which in turn helps to keep that troublesome right shoulder in check. The action of pulling the butt of the handle down towards the ball also encourages the right elbow to stay close to the body in the downswing and this helps to keep the club head travelling on an in-to-out swing path.

Think 'swing through' rather than 'hit at'.

Knee behind the ball

O ne of the main problems with understanding the golf swing is the fact that so much of it takes place where you cannot see what is happening. And given the fact that unless someone comes up with a revolutionary new method of swinging the club whereby all is revealed, we are unfortunately stuck with the present system.

That being the case, anything which we can do at the start of our swing to help make the 'hidden' part easier is worth trying and that is why this tip (which has been a great help to me over the years) might also prove helpful to you.

A good shoulder turn is something that I have admired in many top professionals but sadly failed to emulate. For me, there always seemed to be too many other things to concentrate on like grip, ball position etc. As a result I often fall into the trap of assuming that it would happen naturally if everything else was correct, which sad to say is not the case.

One way to help generate a good winding action is to try to ensure that your left knee gets to a position in the backswing where it points behind, rather than directly at the ball. This movement helps me remember to try to make the best turn I can and at the same time ensures that my weight is transferred correctly to my right side.

Pointing my knee at the ball, instead of past it, normally leads to poor weight transfer and promotes little, or no feeling of 'coiling the spring' in the backswing. And with my weight to the right side, I tend to bring my hand and arms into the shot too soon and as a consequence, fail to complete my backswing properly.

Moving the left knee past the ball may well result in the left heel being pulled up off the ground. This is not really a problem unless taken to the extreme when only the toes remain in contact with the turf.

Ensure that your left knee points behind rather than directly at the ball.

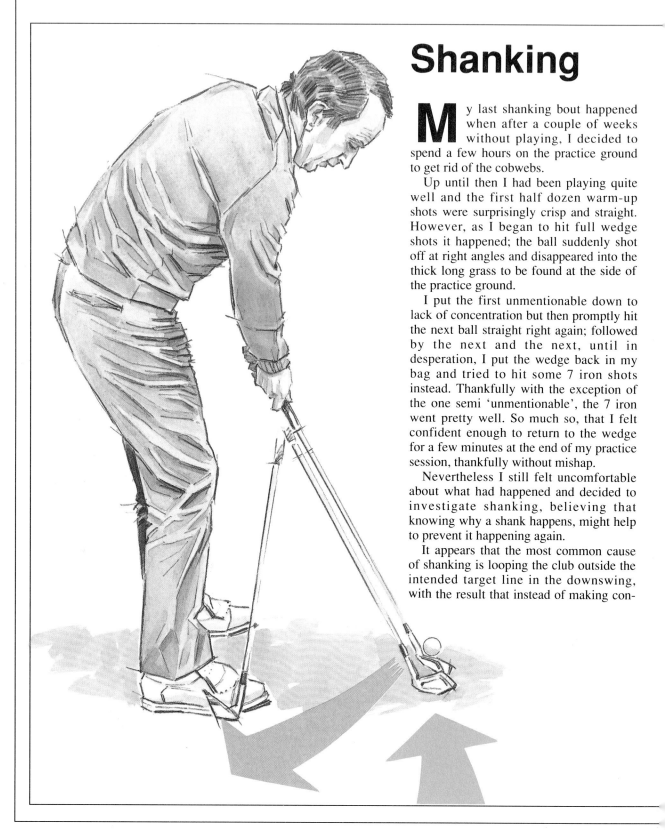

Shanking

My last shanking bout happened when after a couple of weeks without playing, I decided to spend a few hours on the practice ground to get rid of the cobwebs.

Up until then I had been playing quite well and the first half dozen warm-up shots were surprisingly crisp and straight. However, as I began to hit full wedge shots it happened; the ball suddenly shot off at right angles and disappeared into the thick long grass to be found at the side of the practice ground.

I put the first unmentionable down to lack of concentration but then promptly hit the next ball straight right again; followed by the next and the next, until in desperation, I put the wedge back in my bag and tried to hit some 7 iron shots instead. Thankfully with the exception of the one semi 'unmentionable', the 7 iron went pretty well. So much so, that I felt confident enough to return to the wedge for a few minutes at the end of my practice session, thankfully without mishap.

Nevertheless I still felt uncomfortable about what had happened and decided to investigate shanking, believing that knowing why a shank happens, might help to prevent it happening again.

It appears that the most common cause of shanking is looping the club outside the intended target line in the downswing, with the result that instead of making con-

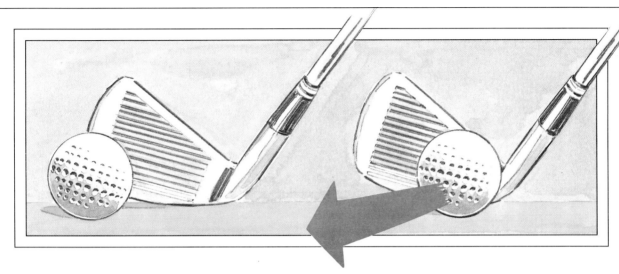

tact with the face of the club, the ball strikes the hosel, or neck of the club. This change in swing path can happen for several reasons, including, trying to steer the ball, or by the weight moving forward onto the toes in the downswing, thereby forcing the arc of the club out of its correct path back to the ball.

In my case, attempting to steer the ball was one of the reasons why I shanked those wedge shots. I had started off hitting the balls in a relaxed manner, then had picked out a target and was trying too hard to hit the mark with every shot. I also discovered that another contributing factor to my bout of the 'unmentionables' was swinging the club back rather too much on the inside.

I had always felt that I hit the ball too high with my wedge and in an effort to lower the trajectory and produce a more penetrating flight, I had flattened the arc of the swing too much, and the results were quite disastrous.

What I had not realised was that my 'flat' swing had caused me to take the club back on the inside. Then, as I returned the club face to the ball, it was so far open that it was impossible to get it square at impact and the ball was struck by the hosel of the club resulting in the dreaded shank.

If you are currently suffering from a bout of shanking, the best advice I can pass on is to book a lesson with your local pro as quickly as possible. He has seen it all before and can recommend the correct treatment for your specific problem.

However, if you fall victim while out on the course, there are one or two 'first-aid' hints that might help you save your sanity and get you back to the clubhouse without any permanent damage.

The first thing to do is to try to think positively about the next shot you have to play, probably with the same club, if you happen to be close to the green. Try to picture yourself playing the shot with a nice smooth rhythm and the ball landing close to the hole. Try to avoid steering the ball, remember that once it leaves the clubface there is nothing you can do about it so play the shot accordingly.

From the technical standpoint, it might help if instead of setting up with the ball positioned in the centre of the clubface, you line it up on the toe of the club.

Also, to guard against taking the club back too much on the inside, try to picture a line running straight between the ball and the hole and concentrate on starting the club back along that straight line.

Most important of all, try to keep your swing smooth and don't be afraid to release your hands through impact. You may not end up next to the pin but hopefully you will hit the green.

(Above left) Lining up with the ball positioned at the toe of the club can help overcome shanking.

(Above right) A shank happens when the ball is struck with the hosel, or neck of the club, instead of the face.

(Opposite) Looping the club outside the target line in the downswing, is a common cause of shanking. A shank can also result through taking the club back too much on the inside and fanning the blade open in the process.

Inside the line

Once upon a time, in the dim and distant past, my natural shot was not a fade but a draw.

This came about, not so much by being taught or by trying to shape the way I hit the ball, but rather, I suspect, by the environment in which I learned to play the game: the windy links courses of my native Scotland.

There, it was usually advisable to keep the flight of the ball as low as possible, in order to combat the wind that could vary from a light breeze to a full force eight gale — all in the time it took to play a single hole. The other benefit that I derived from having a right-to-left shape of shot came from the fact that a low draw will also run quite a good bit further than a high fade.

However, as time passed, I moved away from the coast and found myself playing most of my golf on inland and parkland courses where the wind was not such an important factor. Gradually I began to acquire a slightly more upright swing. After all, there was little to be gained from a low running shot on lush fairways and the demise of the occasional duck hook certainly helped my medal cards.

Now everything would have been fine had I been prepared to accept that my left-to-right swing would not hit the ball as far as my old right-to-left. After all, I was no longer the youthful, three-rounds-a-week golfer that I used to be, nor was I quite as supple of limb or speedy of hand action. But after several years of always being the first in our fourball to play his second shot, I became disenchanted with my safe, if shorter, left-to-right fade and decided to resurrect my old draw action.

I spent the next few weeks hitting a variety of ugly and expensive shots that included pulled short irons, pushed or blocked long irons and woods. An occasional shank threatened to decapitate anyone who happened to be in range at the time. Finally, one of my regular playing partners pointed out the reason for my problem and offered a possible cure.

My problem, it appeared, had stemmed from the fact that in trying to resurrect my old in-to-out swing I had gone too far. I was taking the club back far too much on the inside, from the very start of my swing. As a result of getting too much inside in the backswing, I was unable to clear my left side properly in the downswing.

The cure suggested was in two parts. The first concerned a practice drill whereby I hung an old car blanket over the washing line in my back garden. I then took up my normal address position in front of the washing line but standing far enough away from the blanket to allow me to swing back on the correct line without the head of the club hitting the blanket. If on the other hand, I started back too much on the inside, the clubhead would hit the blanket and I would be aware that I had fallen back into bad habits.

The practice sessions worked well and I was soon back on the right path, at least as far as my backswing was concerned. However, I am pretty sure that the laws of the game would frown upon me marching round the course with blanket and washing line, and here the second part of my cure came into play.

On the golf course I imagined that every time I set up to play a normal shot, I was standing a few feet in front of a brick wall and that as long as I stayed on the correct path in my backswing I would not smash my nice, shiny clubs in the wall. After a few holes I was comfortable again and found myself occasionally playing my foursome second shots last, instead of first.

In a bid to regain my skill of drawing the ball I made the mistake of taking the club back far too much on the inside from the very start of my swing. By getting too much inside on the backswing, I was unable to clear my left side properly in the downswing.

Hips allowed to turn too much and too soon in the backswing, make it impossible to wind the spring properly.

Hitting from the top

Hitting from the top is another swing problem many weekend golfers suffer from and it does not only happen when we have the driver in our hands. It can occur with most clubs in the bag, as I once discovered during a troublesome spell with my middle irons.

At first, I thought the problem stemmed from the fact that I was not taking enough club, which was causing me to force the shot, in order to achieve the required distance. However, this theory was quickly discarded when the problem persisted, even when I was taking more club than was necessary.

As usual, when you are experiencing a problem with your game, there was plenty of well meaning advice on hand, mainly from the bandits who take money from me every Sunday morning.

However it took an hour of sweating and swearing on the practice ground to find the solution and eventually, by a process of trial and error, I finally realised what I had been doing wrong.

My hitting from the top problem had been caused by allowing my hips to turn too much in the backswing and as a result, I was unable to create the proper winding action with the top half of my body. And without this coiling action, which I can best describe as like winding a spring, there was virtually no power being generated in the backswing.

Therefore, in a vain effort to generate power in the downswing, I was hitting at the ball with my arms and hands.

However, by restricting the amount of hip turn, I was once again able to create the 'coiling' action in the backswing and this allowed me to release that tension, or power, properly in the downswing; allowing the clubhead to accelerate naturally and smoothly. This also encouraged my legs to work in harmony with my arms and contributed to producing the power and balance which had been missing when I was hitting from the top.

Once I had sorted out the problem, I remembered a tip that could have saved me muddling about in the dark on the practice ground. It had worked for me at that time and it might help you if you suffer from this particular problem.

A friend suggested that I concentrated on the top half of my body in the backswing by restricting my hip turn, and to emphasize the feeling of winding the spring by making as full a shoulder turn as possible, without injuring myself!

Then when it came to the downswing, I should try to reverse this procedure. This time putting the emphasis on the bottom half of my body by using my legs, not just to transfer my weight back onto my left side, but also to help clear my hips to the left and to allow my arms to swing the club smoothly down and through towards the target.

By restricting the hip turn, the top half of the body winds the spring fully and builds up power which can then be released in the downswing where the legs take over the dominating role.

A dip in form

One of the great pitfalls in trying to improve my golf is the way in which by attempting to cure one fault, I inevitably inherit another.

I was once hacking my way around our local course, getting more and more frustrated with how little distance I seemed to be getting from all my shots. There seemed to be no power in my driving and there was a complete lack of zip in my iron play. The harder that I tried to hit the ball, the worse I became and it was not until I had hit my tee shot out-of-bounds at a par three hole, and therefore had time to think while walking to the next tee, that I believed I had found the answer to my problem.

I convinced myself that I had been concentrating too much on hand action and, as a result, was forgetting to use my legs in the swing. That, I believed, was the reason for my lack of distance and for the absence of crispness in my iron shots. On the next hole I put my theory to the test; to my surprise it worked. The ball flew long, if not exactly arrow straight down the fairway. And for the remainder of the round the spring came back into my step and all was once again right in the world.

Over the following few weeks I continued to concentrate on getting more leg action into my swing and although I hit the occasional slightly fat shot, I was getting my old distance again from the tee. Unfortunately, the fat shots started to become a regular feature of my round. From someone who previously used to gently brush the turf with iron shots, I had began to leave huge gaping craters in the turf, and that was with my fairway woods!

I would like to be able to tell you that I worked out the solution to my new problem by careful thought and detailed swing analysis. However, if the truth be known, the answer was provided by the sun; or rather the shadow cast by my body on a sunny day. I had gone to the club to see if the local pro could sort me out, only to remember as I got out of the car that it was his day off. I decided that having come to the club I might as well spend half an hour on the practice ground. It was a nice sunny day and perhaps things might just take a change for the better; they didn't. There I was still digging great clods out of the practice tee and getting nowhere, except closer to the centre of the earth, when I noticed that as I swung the club, the shadow that I was casting on the turf seemed to be dipping as I swung through the shot.

Could this, I wondered, be the reason for my current attempt to excavate half the county of Cambridgeshire? I made a few tentative practice swings, still keeping my legs active but trying to avoid dipping into the shot. Feeling less than confident about the outcome, I decided to put my latest theory into practice and to my great relief it worked successfully.

No longer was I catching the turf fractionally behind the ball; instead I was striking the ball first and then the turf. Trying to use my legs had not caused the problem, it was the dipping action that I had developed through trying to emphasize my leg action that proved to be the culprit.

At address and through to the top of the backswing, things went according to plan. However, as I swung the club down towards the ball, I must have subconsciously been exaggerating the drive from my legs and this caused me to dip. This led to me losing height and effectively lowered the arc of my swing, and the clubhead was contacting the ground before it reached the ball in the downswing.

Now I concentrate on clearing my left side in the downswing by turning my hips to the left around a firm left leg to prevent the return of the dreaded dips.

Exaggerated leg action can lead to loss of height in the downswing.

Chin up

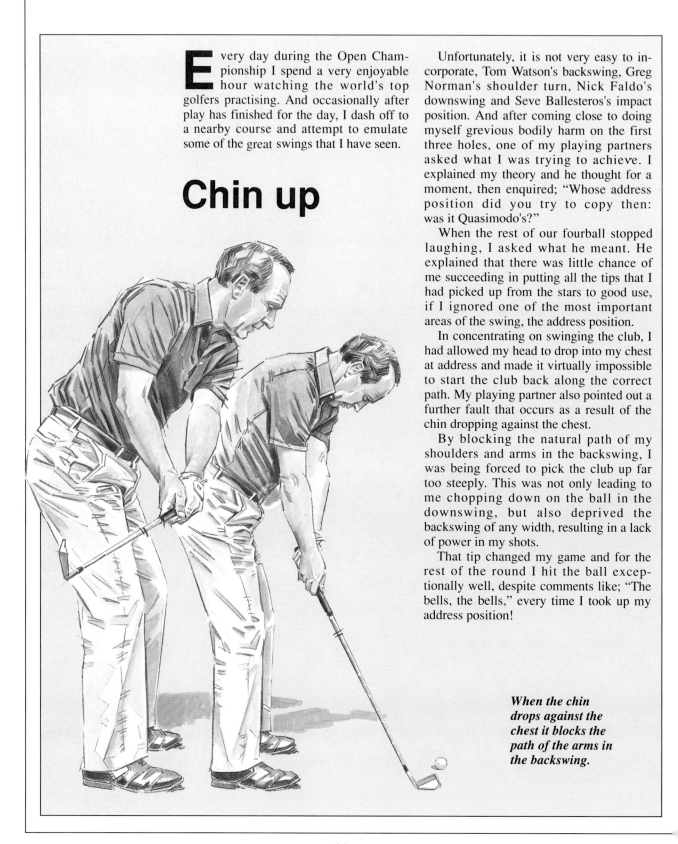

Every day during the Open Championship I spend a very enjoyable hour watching the world's top golfers practising. And occasionally after play has finished for the day, I dash off to a nearby course and attempt to emulate some of the great swings that I have seen.

Unfortunately, it is not very easy to incorporate, Tom Watson's backswing, Greg Norman's shoulder turn, Nick Faldo's downswing and Seve Ballesteros's impact position. And after coming close to doing myself grevious bodily harm on the first three holes, one of my playing partners asked what I was trying to achieve. I explained my theory and he thought for a moment, then enquired; "Whose address position did you try to copy then: was it Quasimodo's?"

When the rest of our fourball stopped laughing, I asked what he meant. He explained that there was little chance of me succeeding in putting all the tips that I had picked up from the stars to good use, if I ignored one of the most important areas of the swing, the address position.

In concentrating on swinging the club, I had allowed my head to drop into my chest at address and made it virtually impossible to start the club back along the correct path. My playing partner also pointed out a further fault that occurs as a result of the chin dropping against the chest.

By blocking the natural path of my shoulders and arms in the backswing, I was being forced to pick the club up far too steeply. This was not only leading to me chopping down on the ball in the downswing, but also deprived the backswing of any width, resulting in a lack of power in my shots.

That tip changed my game and for the rest of the round I hit the ball exceptionally well, despite comments like; "The bells, the bells," every time I took up my address position!

When the chin drops against the chest it blocks the path of the arms in the backswing.

Beat the slice

One of the weekend golfer's greatest problems, especially with the driver, is hitting from the top. This action usually encourages the right shoulder to dominate the downswing and can lead to the clubhead travelling on an in-to-out swing path which produces that ugly slice.

The problem is, how to prevent that right shoulder coming in too soon because of the desire to hit it rather than swing the head of the club through the ball and on towards the target. If you suffer from this affliction there is a way that you could overcome it: give the mind something else to think about; in this case, your belt buckle. As you address the ball concentrate on the image of your belt buckle pointing at right angles to the target line. Then before you start your backswing try to paint a mental picture of your buckle facing directly towards the target as you swing through to a full follow through position. Concentrating on the buckle will help make the bottom half of your body the dominant factor in the downswing, relegating the top half, and that troublesome right shoulder, to a secondary role.

Your belt buckle can help you to beat the slice and prevent the right shoulder coming in too soon.

Swing triggers

One of my many faults is thinking about too many aspects of the golf swing at the same time as attempting to hit the ball. Is my grip too strong? Am I tending to stand too open or too closed? Have I picked the club up too steeply in the backswing?

The result of this mental mish-mash is usually a disjointed start to the backswing where most of the moving bits start off independently and seldom, if ever, become properly integrated throughout the remainder of the swing. The resulting shots normally fly everywhere, except in the intended direction.

Ideally, the swing should start with everything working in unison but that is not always as easy as it sounds. However, there are one or two tricks of the trade, as they say, which I try out from time to time when my swing becomes disjointed.

The first of these two swing triggers is called the 'Forward Press'. I take up my normal address position with my hands level with the ball. Then, instead of taking the club straight back, I press my hands slightly to the left and then start the club back. This seems to help me gather together swing components such as weight transfer and shoulder turn, and get them working together in the backswing.

Another trigger which sometimes works for me, is the old Gary Player tip of starting the backswing by 'kicking' the right knee towards the target. Once again I take up the normal address position but then, instead of starting the club straight back with the hands and arms, the right knee is pressed towards the target. Then, almost as a rebounding action, the right leg moves back to the right and acts as the key to stimulating the other components of the backswing into synchronized action.

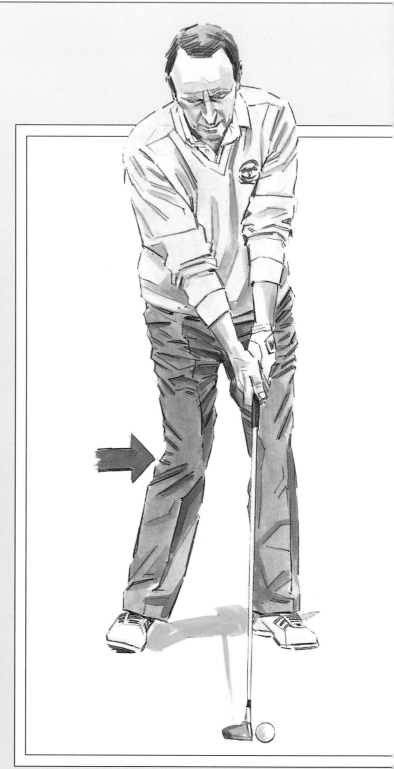

Two swing triggers which have worked for me in the past are: (opposite) kicking the right knee towards the hole before starting the club back and (left) a forward press with the hands helps to get all the moving parts of the swing working together in the backswing.

The writing is on the ball

One fault to which I used to be particularly prone was getting ahead of the ball in the downswing. In my case, it was my head that was moving too quickly in the downswing. Moving your head fractionally is not a major problem in itself. However, when the rest of the body moves with it, then you are in trouble.

'Keep your eye on the ball', is one of the best known of all the old golfing adages, which is probably why it is the one we most frequently forget. I knew that my head was moving but I could not find a way to ensure that this movement was kept to a minimum.

Then I remembered an old putting tip that had been devised to stop head movement. The ball is positioned in such a way as to make sure that the manufacturer's name or logo was visible, only on the area of the ball which makes contact with the clubface. The golfer then concentrates on watching the blade of the putter strike the lettering on the ball.

I adapted this idea by substituting a driver for the putter. Obviously, it is impossible to actually see the face of the driver hit the back of the ball, because the head of the driver travels much faster than that of the putter. However, keeping my eye on the writing on the ball, both as I swing back and then through, helped me keep my head behind the ball at impact.

That is all very well you say when it comes to playing a tee shot or a putt, where you can place the ball to suit you, but what happens through the fairway when you have to play the ball as it lies?

I never claimed that I had found the perfect cure!

Seriously, although I still have the occasional lapse in this department, keeping my eye on the back of the ball is becoming more and more second nature to me now, even when I don't have the writing on the ball to remind me.

And it is an exercise that I would recommend to any golfer who suffers from the problem of getting ahead of the ball in the downswing.

Keeping your eye on the writing on the ball keeps the head behind the ball at impact.

The long and the short of it

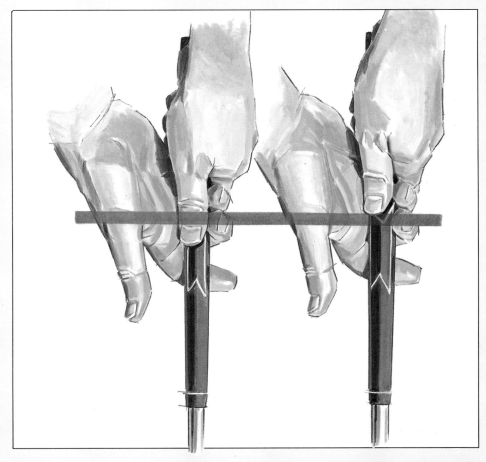

Moving your thumb, either up or down the handle, can change the shape of your shots.

Next time you develop a hook or a slice while playing a round, try this tip which was passed on to me years ago by a crafty old club golfer who always took delight in relieving me of my hard earned cash, during our wagers.

What has always appealed to me about this specific tip is that you can try it out during the round without having to make any major changes to your swing.

If you suddenly find that nice, controlled fade has become a soul-destroying slice, then try moving the thumb of your left hand slightly further up the grip. If hooking is the problem, move the thumb down the handle. In the case of a slice, moving the thumb further up the grip will encourage you to hold the club more in the fingers, which in turn promotes a more active hand action and helps get rid of the slice.

Moving the thumb further down the handle, helps firm-up the grip and encourages a less active hand action which in turn, will help to cure a hook. At this point I must stress the fact that both these tips are more a form of on-course 'first aid', than a permanent cure for hooking or slicing. If the problem continues, then book a lesson with your local club professional who will help you to fully eradicate the fault.

Press forward, to move back

Perhaps the swing fault which plagues we amateur golfers more than any other is rushing the backswing. My own theory is that the problem stems from our unwillingness to accept that you don't have to swing the club back at 100 mph to hit the ball a long way. And it is our preoccupation with length that is the main contributing factor in our failure to achieve it, with any consistency. This problem is perfectly illustrated in the story about the young rookie and the seasoned old professional.

After flashing away at the ball for some 15 minutes, the youngster asked why he was unable to achieve neither length nor accuracy. The pro thought for a minute, then said: "Why don't you try hitting the ball with your backswing."

A touch caustic perhaps, but the message was clear. If we accept that the backswing is merely the means of getting the club into a position from which it can be accelerated back down through the ball, why then do we try to swing the club back at the same speed as we swing it through?

The fact is, that the slower the takeaway, the better your chance of hitting a ball a long way. That's a lesson I have learned from bitter experience and a process of trial and error which, at times, has threatened to turn me into both a physical and mental wreck.

The key to developing a smooth, slow backswing, is creating a one-piece takeaway that encourages all the components of the swing to become active in the correct sequence, producing the combination of power and speed essential, to hit the ball both far and straight.

A one piece takeaway gets all the components of the swing working in unison.

FROM TEE TO GREEN

One of the first things that I tried, and that I still use more than any other method of starting the club back, is to feel that I am pushing it away from the ball with my left shoulder and arm. This has the added bonus of helping to keep the clubhead low to the ground for the first few feet of the takeaway. The low backswing encourages a wide swing arc, which is essential if you want to create maximum power in the swing.

Another method to help develop a one-piece takeaway, is the 'forward press'. Once you have taken up your address position, the hands are pressed slightly to the left (towards the target). This sets up a 'rebound' action, which helps get all the swing components moving in unison. South African Gary Player has used the forward press with great success throughout his long and distinguished career. Gary has also been known to use another method of initiating his backswing, which is to start the movement by gently kicking his right knee towards the target. This again, is a variation on the 'rebound' theme, and you may find it works for you.

Finally, you might like to try a method which is favoured by Jack Nicklaus, Greg Norman and Scotland's Sam Torrance. With this method the clubhead is held fractionally above the ground, instead of being allowed to sit on the turf behind the ball. By holding the club in this manner Jack, Greg and Sam feel that it is easier to make a smooth and controlled start to their swing and avoiding the tendency to pick up the club too steeply from the ground in the backswing.

Thumbs up

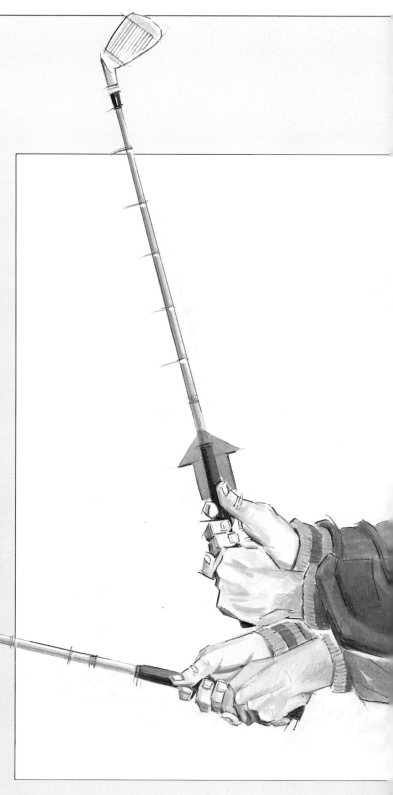

I have long been a fan of the Australian golfer, Greg Norman. The 'Great White Shark' as he is nicknamed, is certainly one of the most exciting players in the game today and his attacking style of play has made him a big favourite with golfers all over the world. Greg also hits the ball prodigious distances, which is why I decided to try and copy his swing — with disastrous results!

To me, one of the keys to Norman's power was the width of his swing. I had noticed how low he keeps the driver to the ground as he sweeps it back from the ball. And how wide an arc he develops as a result. So far, so good, but it was at this point that things started to go wrong.

In my efforts to create a wide arc, I had made a determined effort not to allow my wrists to cock until the club had reached around hip height in my backswing — or so I thought. I spent the next couple of

It's a good thing to get as much width in your swing as possible, but not if it impedes your wrist cock. A good tip is to get the thumbs pointing up, not straight out, in the backswing.

rounds flailing away at the ball, getting more and more frustrated. For not only was I getting nowhere near the extra distance I had expected to achieve with my new swing, to my annoyance, I found that I was hitting the ball even shorter than I did with my old swing.

As usual when I get too carried away with the theory of the golf swing, it takes a visit to my local club professional to get me back on the rails again. The problem had not stemmed from my basic belief that a wide arc could help me hit the ball further, but rather from the way I had tried to set about achieving this.

Not permitting my wrists to break until they reached waist height certainly helped to produce a wide arc. Unfortunately, I had carried this idea too far, and had reached a point where I had not only shortened my backswing too much, it also robbed my downswing of the uncocking action of my wrists which contribute so much in creating power through hand speed.

Because my backswing had become too short and I had no proper wrist cock, I was attempting to generate power from my shoulder and arms, which led to a slice with the long clubs and a low pull to the left with the short irons. There was nothing wrong in trying to establish a good wide arc in the backswing, provided that it did not lead to me swaying too much or overbalancing. The problem now was to cure me of that nasty habit of not cocking my wrists.

My pro came up with a novel solution to the problem by asking me to practise thinking 'thumbs up' as I took the club back. This had the effect of encouraging me to cock my wrists properly, while at the same time, encouraging me to create a good, wide arc in my backswing.

Feet first

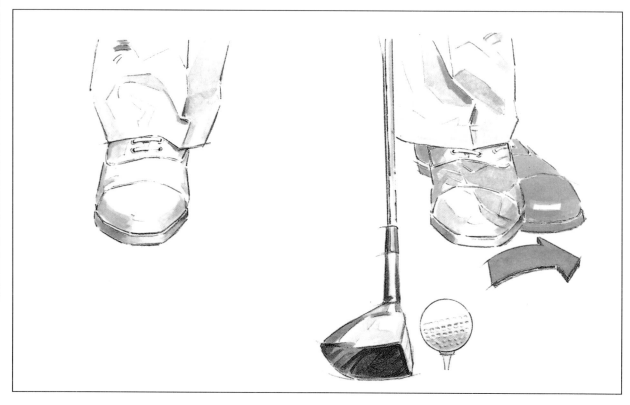

One of the problems which we amateur golfers suffer from is failing to clear the left side properly in the throughswing, especially when it comes to the woods and to the long irons.

It is a fault that can lead to several swing errors, including slicing, pushing and in some cases skying. You might be surprised to discover that the fault can often be traced not to the swing, but to the feet, or rather the position of the feet.

During an Ian Woosnam golf clinic that I once attended at Patshull Park near Wolverhampton, where the Welshman is the Director of Golf, one of the gallery of enthralled spectators asked Ian why he had his left foot turned open at address.

Ian pointed out that many amateur golfers fall into the trap of positioning both feet at right angles to the target line when they address the ball. And although he stressed the importance of the right foot

positioned square to the target, he demonstrated how, by opening the left foot slightly, it encouraged the body to move freely through the shot, creating more power and better and longer shots.

According to Ian, when the left foot is positioned square instead of slightly open, it can act as a barrier to proper weight transfer and the type of bad shots which can result from this fault. It was a brilliantly simple tip and I can vouch for how well it works.

And it most definitely works for Ian Woosnam as he demonstrated to his clinic audience, by hitting a series of driver shots from the fairway. With the wind blowing directly at his back and standing on a slope and with his feet several inches above the ball, the Welshman hit a series of perfect shots, miles down the centre of the fairway with just a touch of draw!

Turning the left foot into a slightly open position at address can encourage a better weight transfer through the shot.

CHAPTER THREE

Grips

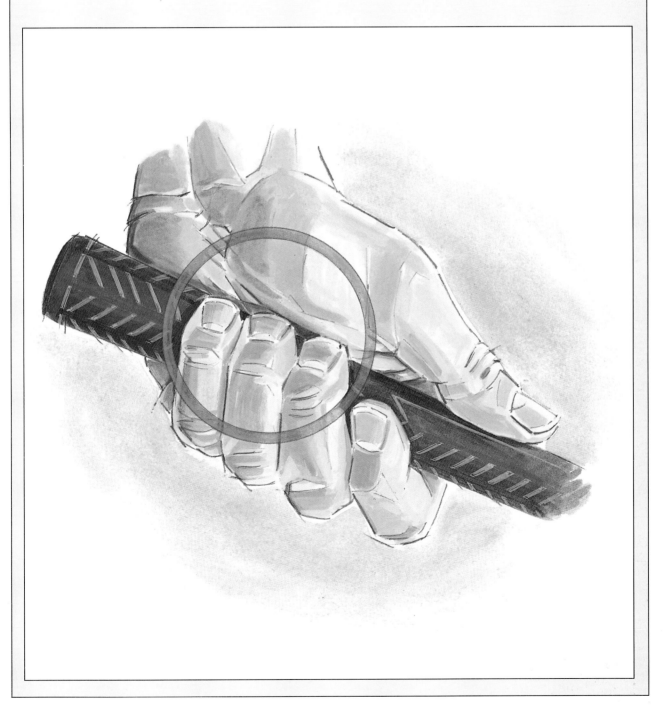

Seeing is believing

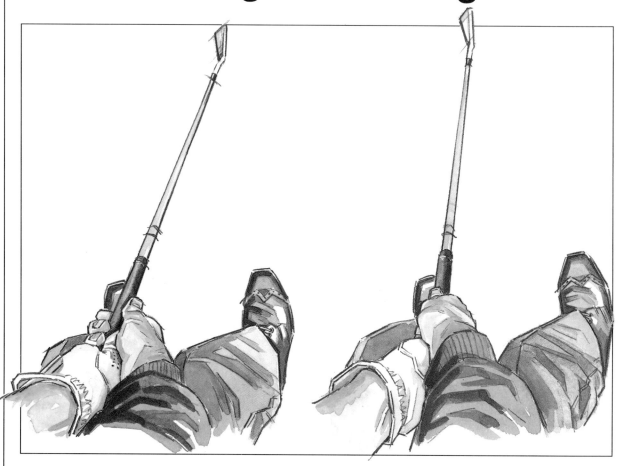

There is no doubt that without a proper grip, you will not get far in golf. A good swing and a supple body will not compensate and although you might find a way of hitting the ball with reasonable consistency, you will always be fighting a fault.

The problem with checking your grip is similar to checking the length of your backswing; you cannot see what is happening at the top of the swing when your hands are usually behind your head. This is the position where any flaws in your grip will really come to light, because the grip, to a great extent, influences the direction in which the face of the club will be pointing and a hook or a slice can result just as much from a poor grip as from a poor swing.

One way to avoid errant shots as the result of a bad grip, is to make sure you are gripping the club correctly at address. In order to do this properly it is important to remember that it is what you see looking down on your hands (as illustrated above) that counts, not what a well-meaning partner might see looking at your grip from directly opposite of your hands as they are placed on the club.

This is because his view is from directly opposite, while yours' is from a position where your head is slightly to the side.

(Above left) TOO MUCH... Golfer's eye shows this grip is too strong with the right thumb against the side of the grip instead of resting on top.

(Above right) TOO LITTLE... This grip is too weak, with the right thumb too far over on top of the grip.

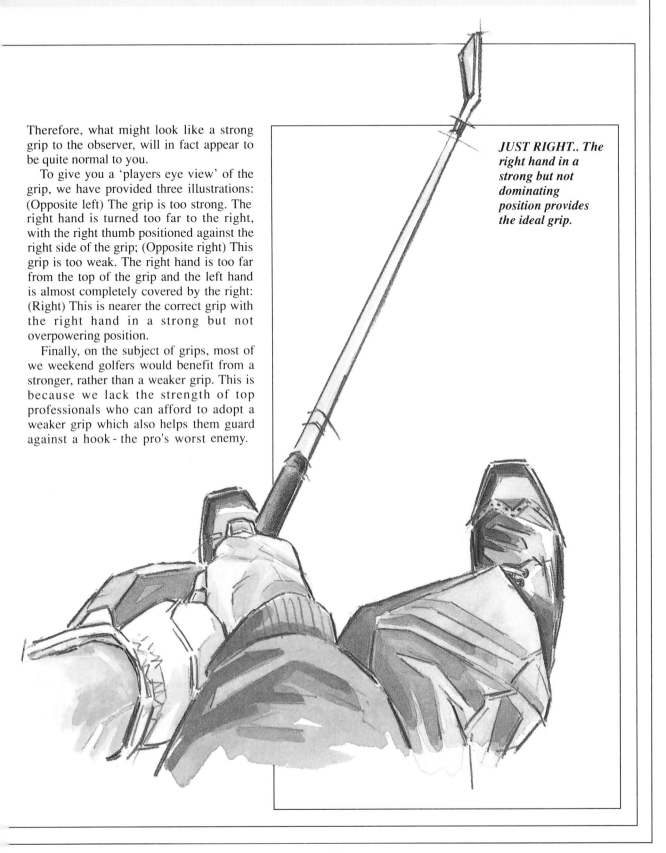

FROM TEE TO GREEN

Therefore, what might look like a strong grip to the observer, will in fact appear to be quite normal to you.

To give you a 'players eye view' of the grip, we have provided three illustrations: (Opposite left) The grip is too strong. The right hand is turned too far to the right, with the right thumb positioned against the right side of the grip; (Opposite right) This grip is too weak. The right hand is too far from the top of the grip and the left hand is almost completely covered by the right: (Right) This is nearer the correct grip with the right hand in a strong but not overpowering position.

Finally, on the subject of grips, most of we weekend golfers would benefit from a stronger, rather than a weaker grip. This is because we lack the strength of top professionals who can afford to adopt a weaker grip which also helps them guard against a hook - the pro's worst enemy.

JUST RIGHT.. The right hand in a strong but not dominating position provides the ideal grip.

GRIPS

Grip check

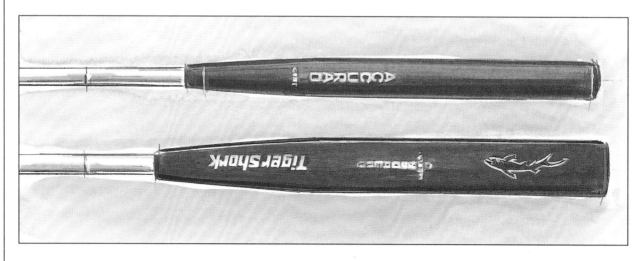

I f your grips have become hard and shiny, this can encourage you to grip the club too tightly which in turn, builds up tension in the wrists and forearms. The swing then becomes stiff and wooden, resulting in poor hand action through the shot.

Although your grips may be in good condition, the same thing can happen if they are too thick. Thick grips tend to produce less active hand and wrist action in the swing and this can result in the loss of both power and accuracy.

However, golfers should also be wary of playing with grips which are too thin because this can encourage excessive hand action leading once again to loss of accuracy and power.

To discover if your grips are the correct size, hold the club in your left hand and take your normal grip. If your grips are correct, the fingers of your left hand should just be able to touch the palm of your hand. If the fingers fail to reach then the grips are too thick. And if the fingers dig into the palm the grips are too thin.

A thicker grip (bottom) is a good cure for missing short putts.

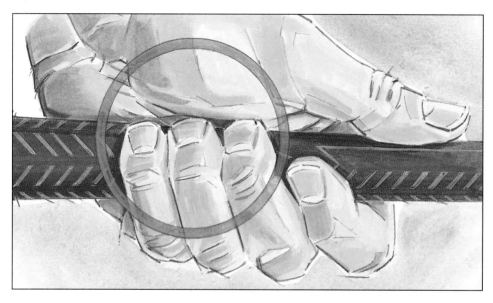

This single grip check will tell you whether or not your grips are the right size.

Self healing

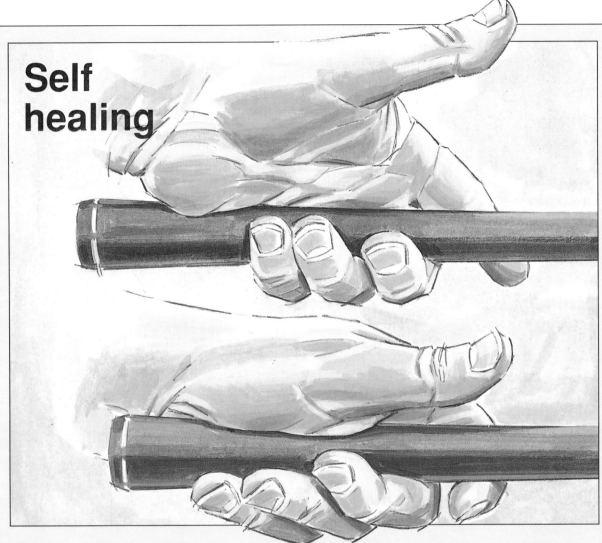

One of the most common grip faults among we amateur golfers is allowing the club to slip into the palm of the left hand, instead of keeping it firmly anchored under the heel of the hand.

It is important (for right-handed golfers) that there is a feeling of strength in the left hand while swinging the club, in order to avoid the right hand becoming too dominant. And there is a simple exercise which demonstrates perfectly the difference in this feeling of strength between the two grips.

First hold a club in your left hand with the grip running across the palm of your hand. Then extend your arm fully and removing your thumb and forefinger from the grip, hold the club horizontally at shoulder height for 10 seconds. I think that you'll discover that there is very little feeling of strength with this grip.

Next, repeat the exercise, but this time make sure that the club is positioned under the heel of the hand and secured by the last three fingers of the hand. This produces a much firmer grip and also promotes a much stronger feeling in the left hand.

The 'palm' grip will not only encourage the right hand to dominate the swing but it can also lead to the club moving out of position at the top of the backswing. The 'heel on top' grip will help to overcome both these problems.

(Top) The club is positioned under the heel of the hand to promote a feeling of strength in the left hand.

(Bottom) When the club is held in the palm of the hand the grip is less able to stop the right hand dominating the shot.

Gripping stuff

Although it is generally accepted that there are three basic methods of gripping the club — Vardon, Interlock and Hammer grip — when it comes to gripping the putter, almost anything goes, provided it gets the ball into the hole.

During a particularly poor spell with the putter at the start of one season, I decided to try out a few different methods of gripping the club before I considered the more drastic step of changing my putter.

Since I first took up the game, I have always used one of the more conventional putting grips; that is, with both thumbs down the centre of the grip and all my fingers on the handle, except for the index finger of my left hand which I positioned vertically, over the top of the fingers of my right hand.

This, with one or two slight variations, is the most common putting grip as it encourages the hands to work best as a single unit. The two handed, or hammer grip, is not quite as common but it does provide the benefit of allowing some golfers to use the same grip for putting, as for hitting the irons and woods.

(Below right) The most common putting grip with the index finger of the left hand overlapping the fingers of the right hand.

(Below left) The hands together on the handle and both forefingers positioned parallel down either side of the shaft.

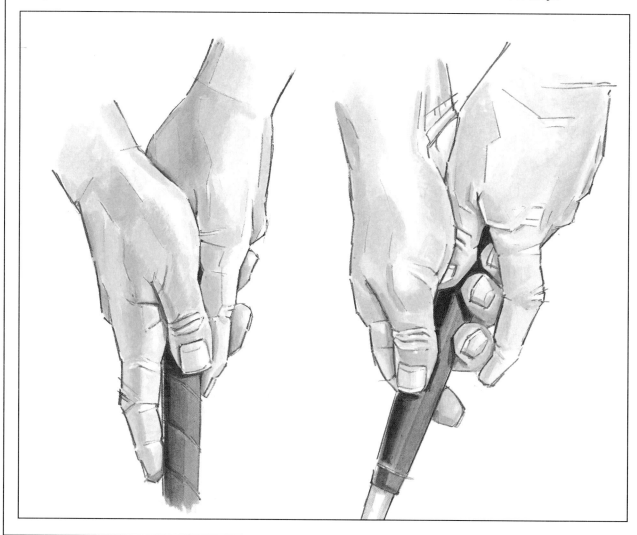

FROM TEE TO GREEN

More and more golfers, including some of the top stars like Mark McNulty, are now adopting a grip which has both thumbs positioned on top of the grip and both forefingers, parallel, down the side of the grip.

Apart from these three recognized methods of gripping the putter, there are several other variations which have found favour, both with club golfers and top pros alike. Denis Durnian, one of the best putters on the European tour, uses a split-hand method in which all the fingers of both hands are on the handle. There is a definite space between the hands, with the forefinger of the right hand resting on the metal of the putter shaft at the point where it meets the bottom of the grip.

The most famous 'new' grip to appear on the golfing scene in recent years is the 'left under right' style which Bernhard Langer adopted to help him conquer the dreaded yips. With this grip, the normal position of the hands is reversed, with the right hand positioned at the top of the handle and the left underneath.

This grip seems to help counter the yips, especially on shorter putts, strengthening

(Below left) The type of grip often favoured by Bernhard Langer to prevent the dreaded 'yips' causing him problems on short putts.
(Below right) This type of grip is designed to take any hand or wrist action out of the putting stroke.

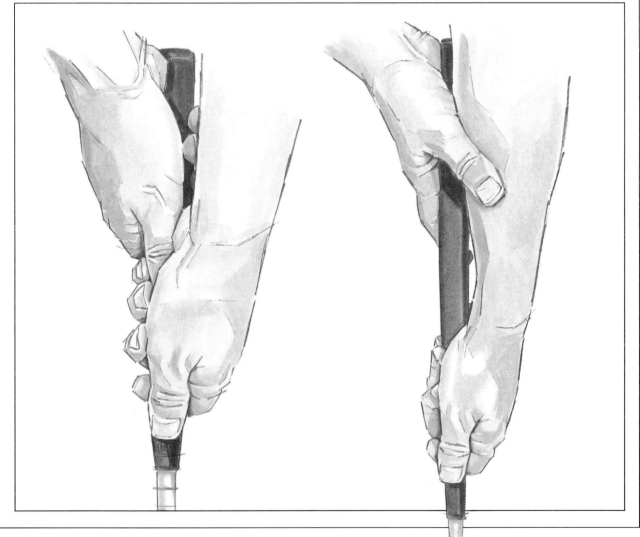

Gripping stuff

the role of the left hand, which leads the putter through the stroke. Bernhard has since introduced another variation to this method with the grip of the putter held against the inside of the left forearm and locked into position with the right hand.

The objective of this putting grip is to take all hand action out of the stroke, which is made with the arms and with the shoulders.

I confess to having tried out most of these putting styles and I did find that the left hand under right grip worked remarkably well, especially on those nasty three footers. But in the end, putting is, in my humble opinion, more about confidence than technique and I have now come full circle back to my original method; at least until the next new method, guaranteed never to miss from three feet, emerges.

(Below left) The hammer style putting grip which has all ten fingers on the handle and which allows some golfers to use the same grip for putting as for normal shots.

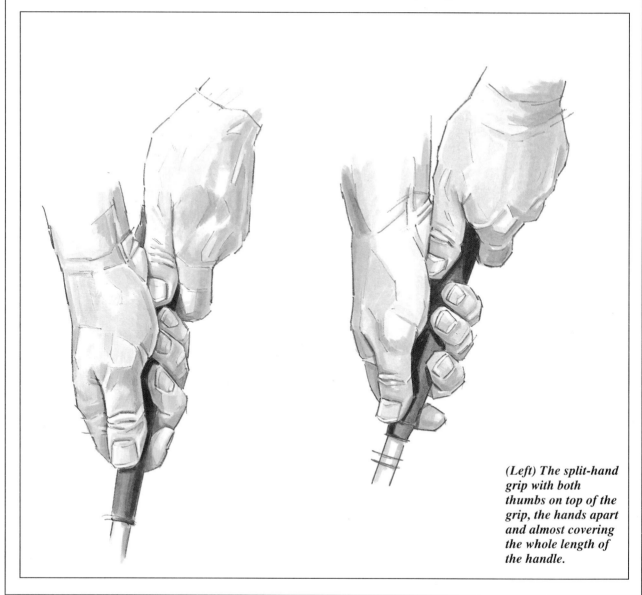

(Left) The split-hand grip with both thumbs on top of the grip, the hands apart and almost covering the whole length of the handle.

CHAPTER FOUR

The fairway

Lady luck and the fairway wood

The first priority when playing from the rough, should be to get the ball back on the fairway by the simplest and most direct route. Then, depending on factors such as depth of the rough, type of lie, line and distance from the green, you can decide the kind of shot to play.

There are times when the best you can hope for is to hack the ball out with a sand wedge. However, occasionally, Lady Luck smiles on you and when that happens, every golfer, regardless of ability, should be ready to take proper advantage of their good fortune.

Let's take a hypothetical situation at a par 5 hole where you may have missed the fairway from the tee, but find your ball sitting up nicely in the rough. Given that there is nothing obstructing your line, you should be aiming to get the ball well down the fairway.

Because the ball is in the rough, some golfers automatically reject the choice of a wooden club for the shot, preferring instead to hit a long iron. In some instances, this can be a mistake: firstly, because if the ball is sitting up really well, it is possible for the shallow face of the long iron to actually pass right underneath it or, secondly, because the ball will only make contact with the top edge of the clubface, resulting in a shot which simply pops up into the air and goes nowhere. Also if the grass is long, it can wrap itself around the head of an iron club, turning it out of line, and sending the ball off in the wrong direction.

With a fairway wood however, the head of the club will slide through the grass more easily, resulting in a straight shot. But a word of caution; if you do play a wood from the rough, remember to hold the club level with the height of the ball in the grass. If you ground the club behind the ball it could lead to a skied shot and you might even find yourself penalized if,

by grounding the club, you cause the ball to move, before starting your swing.

Don't strive for distance with this type of shot. It is far more important to keep your eye on the ball and try to make a smooth swing through the ball and on to a full finish.

If the ball is sitting up well in the rough, consider using a fairway wood.

Underclubbing

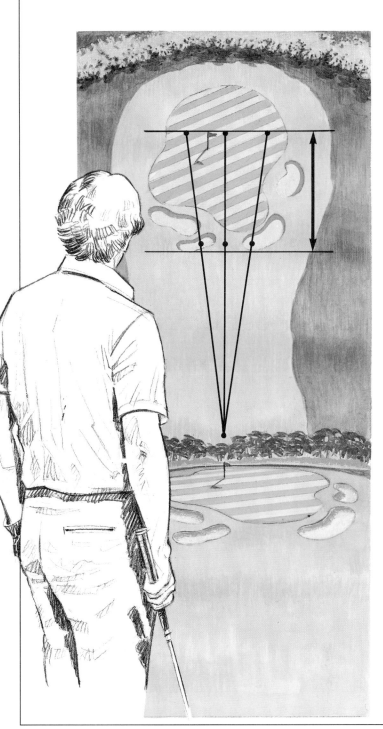

One of the biggest mistakes that golfers make when playing from the fairway to the green, is underclubbing.

Next time you are weighing up this type of shot, ask yourself: 'When was the last time I hit the ball past the flag?'

In the main, most of the trouble around the putting surface is found in front of rather than behind the green, with bunkers and water hazards usually positioned to catch the miss-hit or underclubbed approach shot. Therefore, if you have any doubt regarding the distance you have to carry the ball, choose the longer, rather than the shorter club, for two reasons.

Firstly, with the longer club, if you do push or pull the shot slightly, it will still travel far enough to carry the trouble in front of the green, yet still stay on the putting surface, leaving you with a putt rather than a bunker shot — or worse. And even if you just miss the green, or the ball rolls off the edge of the putting surface, chances are you will still have a reasonable lie and the opportunity of chipping the ball close to the hole.

Secondly, feeling confident that you are playing enough club, will encourage a slow, smooth swing, resulting in a better strike than you might achieve by forcing a shorter club.

Finally, there is nothing more frustrating than hitting a perfect shot straight at the flag only to see the ball finish short of the green because you have underclubbed.

Underclubbing is a very common mistake when playing from the fairway to the green.

Aiming

Agood swing and a solid contact count for nothing if you are not aiming in the right direction. This is something that I have found out to my cost on too many occasions.

Often when I have managed to make a reasonable pass at the ball, my joy has usually been short lived as I have stood there posing in a well balanced follow through, only to see the ball miss the green, more often by yards than feet, thanks to poor aiming.

Now the way I play, I cannot realistically expect to produce a good swing with every shot but there is no reason why I shouldn't be able to at least point myself in the right direction. However, in my defence, aiming correctly is not quite as simple as you might think and even the top stars occasionally stray from the true path: which is one of the reasons why they are usually so meticulous when it comes to setting up prior to playing a shot.

The great Jack Nicklaus, for example, has always been very particular about his alignment when it comes to aiming. So much so, that he has schooled himself to go through a pre-shot routine before he even starts to think about hitting the ball; and he does this whether he's hitting a vital shot in a tournament, or simply warming up on the practice tee.

Well, if it is good enough for Jack Nicklaus, I decided that it was good enough for me, so last week I set out for the practice ground to see if I could work out my own pre-shot aiming routine. To be honest, I had intended to use my usual 'trial and error' routine but crossing the railway line between the car park and the practice ground reminded me of something that I had seen a tournament pro doing while he was practising.

As I watched, the player concerned took two clubs out of his bag and laid them parallel on the ground. Standing directly

SQUARE STANCE
Feet, hips and shoulders should be parallel to the target. They should not point directly at it.

FROM TEE TO GREEN

behind him, I could see that the club furthest from the golfer was pointing directly at a flag in the distance, which I assumed was his intended target. The other club was positioned across the line of his toes, as he took up his address position and as that club was parallel to the other one, it meant that his feet, hips and shoulders, were not in fact pointing at the target, but along a line parallel to the target.

I then realised that most of my aiming problems stemmed from the fact that I had fallen into the bad habit of not bothering to check the position of my shoulders, hips and feet, but instead concentrated on aiming the clubface at the target. Over a

period of time, I had started to align my body to the target as well as the clubface at the target, with the result that there was no way I could swing the club along the correct target line, because my body was actually aiming on the wrong line. Half an hour on the practice ground using the two club aiming drill soon got me back on the rails but the bad news was, that by the time I began to hit the ball in the right direction I was swinging so badly that I was ending up well short of the target. Still, I could now get back to playing, confident in the knowledge that now, when I miss-hit a shot, at least I was miss-hitting in the right direction now.

(Above left)
OPEN STANCE
Using the club aiming set-up, it is easy to see if you are on line when it comes to lining-up.

(Above right)
CLOSED STANCE
This was the closed position that I found I was in when aiming.

Curing miss-hit shots

Although there are many reasons for miss-hitting shots from both the tee and the fairway, when it comes to direction the problems can often be traced to the position of the left wrist at the top of the backswing.

Picture (A) shows the ideal position from which to produce a square hit with the back of the left wrist, the hand and the full arm all forming a straight line and all on the same plane.

Picture (B) is known as the 'arched' position and usually leads to the clubface being returned to the ball in a closed position resulting in a hooked shot.

Picture (C) shows the wrists in the cocked or open position which is common among many amateur golfers and is also one of the main contributing factors in slicing the ball.

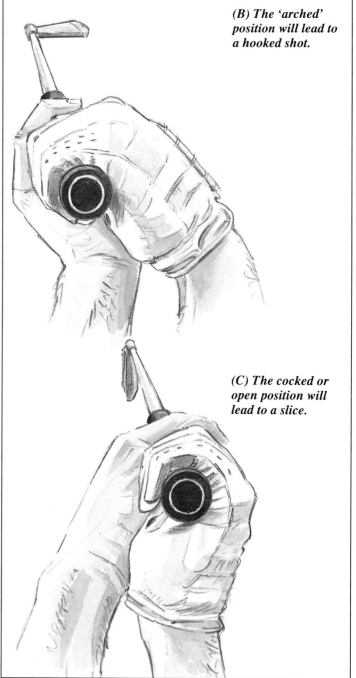

(B) The 'arched' position will lead to a hooked shot.

(C) The cocked or open position will lead to a slice.

(A) The ideal position to produce a correct square hit.

Target practice

I f you get the opportunity to spend a day at a professional tournament this year, then take a tip, and take some time to watch the players hard at work on the practice ground.

You will see lots of different swings but one thing all the top players have in common is the care taken over lining up or aiming. Most pros go through a set routine before hitting a shot and they follow this religiously, even on the practice tee. And justifiably so, because no matter how much power is generated, unless the player is lined up correctly, that power is wasted if the ball flies wide of its intended target.

The routine that many of the top stars follow is something which the average club golfer can easily copy, and involves the following steps.

Having selected the required club, stand directly behind the ball to establish the correct ball to target line. Then pick a spot, perhaps a leaf on the fairway, a few feet in front of the ball and directly on the target line. You will probably find it easier to relate to that object than a distant flag.

The next step is to set the feet, hips and shoulders all parallel to each other. The body should be aiming fractionally left of the target with the shoulders and hips in a slightly open position and the left foot drawn fractionally back from the target line.

This slightly open position helps to encourage the correct in-to-out swing path and to promote a full swing through towards the target.

If the shoulders and hips were pointing right of the target, in a closed position, this would tend to block the left side and hinder the arms from swinging the club through on the correct target line.

One of the main problems when it comes to aiming happens when the golfer attempts to aim both the clubface and the body at the target. This can lead to shots finishing consistently right of the target,

with the result that the golfer starts trying to pull the shot to the left to get the ball back on line. Eventually this leads to shots ending up well left of target leaving the poor golfer in a complete tangle!

Remember, aim the clubface at the target and the body on a parallel, or slightly open line to it.

A good practice and one used quite often by the pros, to check their alignment, is to place two clubs on the ground, one pointing at the intended target, the other laid parallel to the feet to ensure that they are correctly positioned.

It is important to be sure that the feet, hips and shoulders are all parallel to each other. Do not attempt to aim both clubface and body at the target.

Fairway bunkers

There are two major factors to be considered when it comes to playing from a fairway bunker and these are; the type of lie and the height of the lip of the bunker.

If the ball is plugged, or has come to rest in a poor lie, then the chances of playing a successful shot really are severely restricted.

Likewise, if the ball has landed near the front of the bunker and the lip of the bunker is fairly high, then once again, the odds are stacked against you.

However, given a good lie and enough distance between the ball and the lip of the bunker, there is a tried and tested technique for playing a successful recovery shot that will not only get the ball out of the sand but, with a little luck, thought and application, might just enable you to reach the green and save your par.

Before attempting to play a fairway shot, make sure that your feet are firmly anchored in the sand. Remember, unlike a greenside bunker shot, you will be making a full swing and therefore, a sound footing is essential.

With a fairway bunker shot, the swing will be almost similar to a normal shot played from the fairway, and the last thing you should do is to pick the club up too steeply in the backswing then chop down on the back of the ball. This method might get the ball out of the sand but the distance achieved will be minimal.

However, there are two slight changes that you should make before playing the first shot. First, the ball should be moved slightly more towards the centre of your stance but the hands should remain in their normal position. Moving the ball back in the stance will encourage the hands to stay well ahead of the clubface through impact.

As with any shot, rhythm and pace are the keys to success. So don't think distance, try instead to keep your eyes on the ball, make a smooth swing and let the club take care of the distance.

A final point to remember. When you move the ball back in your stance, at the same time keep the hands well forward. This will have the effect of delofting the club, changing a 5 iron, for example, into a 4. This is important when it comes to considering such factors as; how quickly you have to get the ball airborne and the distance the shot has to travel.

If you are fortunate enough to have a good lie in a fairway bunker, you may be able to reach the green — and save your par.

FROM TEE TO GREEN

Uphill and downhill lies

The key to play from an uphill, or for that matter, a downhill lie, is adopting the correct set-up position, which at times can seem like trying to defy the laws of gravity.

However, given that you are not attempting to play up the North face of the Eiger, you should try to achieve a body position as close as possible to the angle of the slope you are playing from. Unfortunately, in the case of an uphill lie, this would mean that far too much weight would move on to your right side the minute you started to swing the club back. And you would then find it extremely difficult to transfer the weight back to the right side in the downswing.

To overcome this problem, the left leg should flex more than the right at address, with the greater percentage of the body weight also retained over the left hip. This position will enable you to sweep the club away from the ball without overbalancing; it might also help you to retain balance if you made the effort to shorten your backswing just a fraction when playing this specific type of shot.

Flexing the left knee not only helps balance, it also permits the body to be positioned at right angles to the slope and this in turn, helps you to swing through the impact area with the clubhead able to follow the contours of the ground.

The ball should be positioned a little further forward in the stance than normal and remember, although you have made some compensation for both the slope and your balance, there will still be a tendency for the weight to hang back on the right foot as you play the shot. This can lead to the shot hooking to the left rather than flying straight, so compensate for this factor when lining up. Making a definite effort to extend the follow-through will also help to reduce the amount of draw.

When playing from an uphill lie it is essential not to rush your swing. It is difficult enough to retain proper balance without having to cope with sudden and violent changes in direction!

Finally, try to avoid leaning too far to the left at address in order to compensate for the slope. If you do, chances are you will pick the club up too steeply in the backswing which will result in the clubhead digging into the turf behind the ball at impact instead of sweeping through towards the target.

On an uphill lie, flex the left knee more than the right to help build a sound, well balanced base from which to play the shot.

Seaside fairways

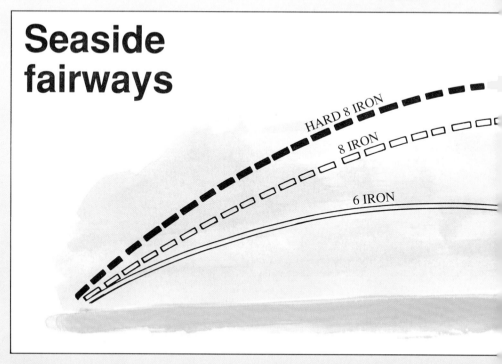

When it comes to playing from the fairway on seaside courses, some golfers, who play on lush inland layouts, find it difficult to get the ball airborne, with the result that they often slice fairway woods and hit iron shots thin.

It is a problem that I also suffer from because when the fairways are firm and the lie appears to be tight, I try to pick the ball cleanly off the surface, instead of hitting down and through as I would do normally.

However, unless the fairways on a links course have been continually baked by the sun (a rare phenomenom in this country) there is little difference between hitting shots from inland or seaside fairways. In fact, more often than not, you will hit a better shot on a links course because the shorter the grass, the better the contact between club and ball.

One way to encourage you to hit down and through when playing from tight fairway lies, is to move the ball back slightly in your stance. In the case of a medium iron, instead of setting up with the ball just inside your left heel, try moving it a couple of inches nearer to the centre of your stance.

It is very much a question of trial and error, but the next time you get the chance to play a links course, try to spare a couple of minutes on the practice ground, finding out the best position to play the ball from in order to achieve the desired results.

The other main problem area, when it comes to playing from hard fairways in windy conditions, is club selection as this is more difficult on a links course because the flatness of the terrain makes it hard to judge distances accurately. Then there is also the question of the type of shot that will produce the best result.

For example, let us assume that you will find yourself approximately 140 yards from the centre of the green. Under normal conditions, on an inland course that shot would call for, let's say, a 7 or 8 iron.

However, on this occasion, you are playing into a fairly stiff breeze and the pin is set at the back of the green.

Your first thought might be simply to hit a harder than normal 8 iron, believing this

FROM TEE TO GREEN

Take more club when playing into the wind instead of trying to hit the ball harder with a more lofted club.

will compensate for the fact that the wind is against. Unfortunately, attempting that type of shot could lead to problems on two fronts. Firstly, as I mentioned earlier, because you are playing from a fairly tight seaside fairway, it is likely that you will make cleaner contact with the ball which will result in producing more backspin, especially in the case of a lofted iron.

This, coupled with the fact that you are hitting into the wind, will make the ball spin ever faster. And the faster it spins, the higher it will fly. All of which means that hitting the shot harder will not necessarily make it travel any further. The second problem stems from the fact that in attempting to hit the ball harder, you are more likely to hurry the shot and could end up hitting behind the ball or thinning it.

The alternative to hitting harder into the wind is in fact to do just the opposite. But, first of all, it is necessary to apply a little basic mathematics. Let us assume that you acquired a course yardage chart from the pro shop and it shows that you are 140 yards from the centre of the green.

The first thing to do is add ten yards for the fact that the pin is at the back of the green, then providing you're not playing into a force 8 gale, add another ten yards to compensate for the wind being against. This means that the shot is now 160 yards and if you apply the rule of thumb which says there is 10 yards difference between each club, that 8 iron shot is now a 6 iron.

Once you have worked out the right club, we come to the difficult bit: having enough conviction to hit a good solid 5 iron when your eye is telling you that you are only an 8 iron distance away.

Here again, a few minutes on the practice ground hitting half a dozen shots into the wind prior to playing will help strengthen your conviction.

One of the best tips I ever had on playing in the wind came from Eddie Birchenough, professional at Royal Lytham and St Annes G.C. Eddie said, "Don't try to hit the ball harder — try to hit it better." And by making sure that you have the correct club in your hand you will quickly discover that the easier you swing, the better the result.

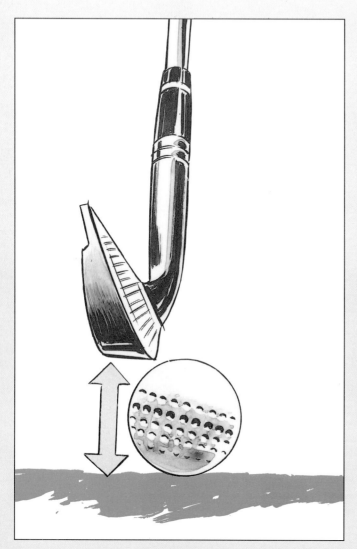

Club above the ball

The best tip I ever received on playing from a fairway bunker, was to hold the club slightly above the ball at address and to focus my attention on the top of the ball rather than the back, as with a normal shot from the fairway.

Holding the club above the ball has two benefits. Firstly, it helps to ensure that as you take the club back it does not touch the sand and cost you a penalty shot. Secondly, it raises the plane of the swing slightly which helps prevent the clubface digging in too deeply behind the ball at impact.

Focus on the top of the ball in a fairway bunker, as you would for a normal fairway shot.

The rough

A ball sitting up in the rough

Recently I had the opportunity to play in a local Pro/Am and for a change played pretty well; unfortunately my fellow amateur team member didn't have such a good day.

I could sympathise with the poor man, because I know how it feels when your game falls apart on the very day you want to be playing your best. What I am sure had been a nice controlled fade only a few days before the Pro/Am, had suddenly become a huge slice and every bounce of the ball seemed to be a bad one.

Still, to his credit, my partner kept plugging away, albeit usually from the waist-deep rough on the right side of the fairway. On the sixth hole, however, it seemed as though his luck had changed for the better. For although he had once again sliced his tee shot into the rough, when we got to the ball, instead of finding it buried, on this occasion it was sitting up on a tuft of grass.

My partner could hardly believe his luck and having worked out that he still had some 150 yards to cover to reach the green, grabbed his 5 iron, hurriedly took up his stance (in case the fates should turn against him again and allow the ball to

topple from its lofty perch) then gave the ball an almighty smash.

Unfortunately, instead of rocketing towards the distant green, the ball climbed almost vertically, arching gracefully over a tall silver birch tree before disappearing into the impenetrable depths of a huge hawthorn bush, never to be seen again.

On the next tee, while we were waiting to play, my partner related his tale of woe to our professional who nodded sympathetically before stepping up and blasting his ball 270 yards down the centre of the fairway. Naturally, our man's ball again found the right hand rough but luckily found a similar lie to the previous hole. However this time the pro was on hand to offer some helpful advice.

He explained that when the ball was sitting up in the rough it was easy to fall into the trap of thinking you had a perfect lie and that could simply whack the ball out. In fact, what often happens is that if you take a normal swing chances are,

because the ball is sitting up so high, it will make contact with only the top half of the clubface, resulting in a loss of power and the ball travelling only a fraction of the intended distance. In some extreme cases the clubhead could actually pass completely under the ball.

To ensure that he got maximum benefit from his good fortune in finding a decent lie in the rough, the pro encouraged our playing partner to set up for the shot with the leading edge of the club aligned with the centre of the ball, instead of attempting to ground the club in the rough behind the ball. By holding the club above ground level it encourages the player to strike the ball first and get it flying forward towards the hole, instead of simply cutting through the grass that the ball is sitting on.

It was a tip that certainly worked on the day and one that, if his slice continues to plague him, my luckless playing partner will undoubtedly have need to call on frequently in the future.

(Opposite) When the ball is sitting up in the rough, position the club with the leading edge of the blade level with the centre of the ball.

(Above) Addressing the ball with the club positioned at normal height could lead to a miss-hit from this type of lie.

Rough justice

It is a fact of golf that secretly, we all tend to think we're better players than we really are. Every time I hit my tee shot into the rough, and that is pretty frequently, I inevitably start to look for my ball at least 20 yards past the spot where I eventually find it.

The same can be said when it comes to playing certain types of shots. I have seen high handicappers march into knee-deep rough with a fairway wood in their hands, confident that they can pull off a recovery shot that would have the most talented pro reaching for his sand wedge.

The same is true of shots played from heavy rough, close to the green. Not long ago I was guilty of attempting such a shot. The ball was barely visible in deep rough, pin high and about 20 feet from the green. And just to add a little more spice to the shot there was a six foot rise between myself and the green.

Did I attempt the sensible recovery shot to the middle of the green? I did not! Instead I went into my Seve Ballesteros mode, opened the clubface, made a long slow swing which should have slid the clubhead under the ball which in turn would have described a high, graceful arc up onto the green where it would have landed softly and trickled gently down to the hole side.

What in fact happened was the club became entangled in the grass and instead of popping out, the ball disappeared deeper into the rough. I prefer not to go into the gory details of my next four shots; suffice to say I did not make my par.

The lesson to be learned in this type of situation is first and foremost, get the ball out and if possible, somewhere on the putting surface, from where you will have at least a chance of saving par by holing

the putt. The technique for playing from heavy rough to a tight pin position is not all that sophisticated; ignore the flag, aim for the part of the green that you can reach without the aid of divine intervention that will get you out of the rough.

One tip about playing from deep rough, is to close the clubface slightly when addressing the ball. This is to compensate for the grass wrapping round the club as the shot is played and forcing the face open. If you address the shot with the clubface too open, chances are, that by the time it reaches the ball it will have been pulled even further open by the grass and this could lead to a shank.

Grip the club firmly, pick it up steeply in the backswing and then swing down into the back of the ball. Try to avoid the temptation to stab at the shot, as this more often than not leaves the ball where it is. Although this type of shot does not require a full flowing follow through, you should still try to keep the club going through after impact.

Using a sand wedge for this shot can help in two ways. First there is the obvious loft on the face to help get the ball airborne quickly. The weight of the heavy flange on the club will also help drive the clubhead through the grass. Finally, be prepared to take your medicine and play out to a spot on the green, or in some cases a spot close to the green, instead of attempting the one-in-a-million shot.

When playing from deep rough, close the clubface slightly to compensate for the grass wrapping round the club and pick the club up quite steeply in the backswing. Don't attempt anything spectacular. Aim to get out and on some part of the green.

How the grass lies

T rying to get distance from the rough, if you excuse the pun, can sometimes be a case of hit or miss.

There are so many things to consider, factors such as the severity of the rough, type of lie, distance required, obstacles between the ball and the target, wet or dry grass, etc.

However, as a general rule of thumb, when it comes to playing any type of recovery shot from the rough, the aim should be to get as little grass as possible between the clubface and the ball at the moment of impact.

To achieve as clean a contact as possible, the club should be swung on a more upright plane and the take-away should be slightly outside the target line. This will produce a fairly steep out-to-in swing path which will help the club slide more easily through the grass. But it is worth remembering that because the path of the club will be cutting across the ball, the shot is more likely to move from left to right in flight.

Another tip to help control the flight of a long shot from the rough, is to ensure that you take a firm grip of the club. This will help prevent the head twisting as it drives through the long grass.

Once again, think swing not distance. A successful recovery shot from the rough is more likely to result from a smooth swing than a hurried stab.

(Top) With the grass lying in the same direction as your shot, the ball will tend to fly on a lower trajectory and run further when it lands. But (centre) against the direction the ball flies higher and rolls less. With a 'flying lie' (bottom) try to sweep the shot away.

Heavy rough

There are certain places on most golf courses where, if you miss the fairway, just finding the ball is an achievement in itself.

When you find yourself in this type of situation, it is important to accept that the best you can now hope for is to get the ball out of the rough and back into play, by the shortest route possible.

So, having resigned yourself to the fact that any forward progress is impossible, the next step is to select the right club and adopt the correct technique to play a successful recovery shot.

When it comes to trying to extricate yourself from really heavy rough, the best club for the job is usually the sand wedge. Remember, distance is not a factor and the weight of the sand wedge, coupled with its loft and deep face, make it the ideal, heavy duty tool.

The technique for playing the shot is very similar to that of a bunker shot: position the ball back in your stance, break the wrists sharply in the backswing and then, keeping a firm grip, drive the clubhead down and through the grass behind the ball. In really deep rough where the ball might be suspended in the grass above ground level, remember to shorten your grip on the club to compensate.

In an effort to make clean contact with the back of the ball when it is lying in deep rough, many amateur golfers chop down a little too steeply and only succeed in driving the ball even deeper into the rough. In this situation, where the ball is barely visible, keep the swing steep but aim to make contact with the grass a few inches behind the ball with the intention of lifting both grass and ball clear at the same time.

The key points to remember when playing from deep rough are: do not be greedy and try for distance when you know that it is not really on; take the shortest route out of trouble; if you have already decided that you cannot reach the green from the position you are in, why try to pinch a few extra yards and risk leaving the ball in the rough? In deep rough, the grass will tend to wrap around the heel and hosel of the club as it drives through, causing the clubface to close. Therefore you should set up with the clubface slightly open, to compensate for this twisting effect.

Keep the weight mainly on your left side, maintain a firm grip on the club and try to avoid letting the left wrist collapse through the hitting area. And finally... a short prayer probably would not go amiss!

(Below)
Extricating your ball from thick rough calls for a technique similar to that of a bunker shot.

Seventh heaven

One club which has recently found a permanent place in my golf bag is a 7 wood. I'd finally had to come to terms with the fact that I had neither the strength nor the necessary skill to hit a long iron from heavy weight rough, and missing as many fairways as I do, this was putting a great deal of pressure on my short game. Even when I was chipping and putting well, it was nearly always to save par, and not for birdies.

It was during a friendly round at my local club that I discovered the answer to my problem. My partner had been given a 7 wood as a Christmas present and for the first couple of holes he bent my ear about what a wonderful club it was, and how it had changed his game.

As usually happens in these cases, he hit every fairway on the first nine holes and I missed most of them. And when I sliced my tee shot into the rough at the 10th, he suggested I have a go with his 7 wood. I was tempted to tell him what he could do

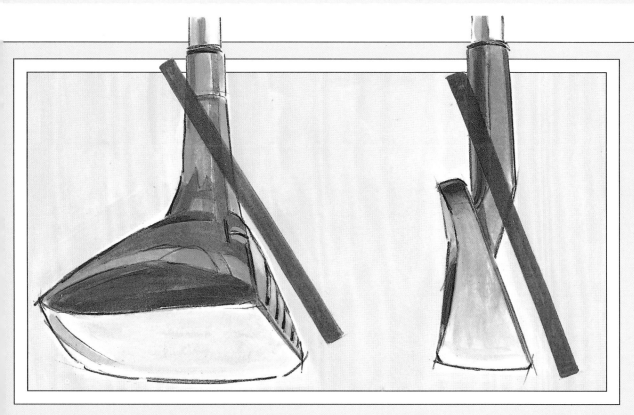

(Above) Note the difference in lift between the 7 wood (left) and the 4 iron (right): an important factor when it comes to getting the ball out of the rough.

with his blessed seven wood, but then decided to give it a try, if only to stop him going on about it.

"Never mind if the lie isn't all that great, the two rails on the sole of the club will cut through the grass and let you get at the back of the ball. You'll be amazed at how easy it is to get the ball up in the air," my partner assured me.

After asking if he had shares in the company who made the club, I took a look at the shot I was facing. The ball could hardly have been described as 'sitting up' but there did appear to be plenty of loft on the face of the club which gave me the feeling that at least I could get the ball airborne.

Before I played the shot, I remembered another tip I picked up about playing from the rough, which concerned establishing a solid base from which to swing. If you allow your weight to get too far back on your heels, it is difficult to keep your balance when playing a full shot from the rough. To stop this happening you should try to imagine that you are digging your toes into the ground. This helps keep your weight on the balls of the feet and encourages an active foot action through the shot.

I held the club slightly further down the grip for better control, tried to make a good shoulder turn and then accelerated the clubhead as smoothly as I could through the ball. The result was amazing. The ball flew cleanly and carried all the way to the green, which was almost 180 yards away.

Unfortunately, my driving didn't improve during the remainder of the round, and I had several further opportunities to try out the 7 wood from the rough. And although I was unable to repeat the spectacular results of the 10th hole, the ball came out cleanly every time and travelled much further than I would ever have managed with a long iron.

(Opposite) The 7 wood gets the ball out of the rough much more easily than a long iron.

Playing rough

Most golfers do not take enough care in selecting the right club when playing from the rough.

Club selection should be determined by the lie; even from quite deep rough, a long recovery shot is still possible, provided that you are lucky enough to find a good lie.

However, a bad lie in heavy rough is a very different proposition and leaves little alternative other than just to get the ball back into play. Avoid the temptation of trying to get too much distance from your recovery shot, especially if it will only mean the difference between hitting a 7 iron rather than a 6 for your third shot.

Instead, take the shortest and safest route back onto the fairway, using a club with which you feel confident of playing a successful recovery shot.

Taking the easy way out is as much for our mental as physical benefit. Trouble shots are the ones which eat away at our reserves of mental energy and whenever possible we should try to avoid these stress situations during a competitive round.

One way to help ease this mental stress is to practise playing recovery shots from all types of hazards. Drop a few balls in the rough and discover just how the ball reacts when you play a recovery shot with different clubs. This will help to relieve some of the mental stress when you find yourself facing that same type of shot in a competitive round.

Tip from Brian Waites, professional at Hollinwell GC Notts, England.

Club selection in the rough is extremely important. Be very careful when assessing your lie.

CHAPTER SIX

Around the green

Short sharp reminder

Not long ago I had been enjoying a rare purple patch with my short game, especially my wedge play, and I was consistently hitting the ball close to the hole, even from the rough.

Unfortunately, my good form did not last and during a recent round my touch with the short irons deserted me completely. Instead of nice, crisp, pitch shots, I began to thin the ball, and when I wasn't sending the ball zooming through the green, I was hitting behind it and flopping shots into greenside bunkers.

Things were becoming so bad that in desperation I asked one of my regular playing partners what I was doing wrong. After some deliberation he replied: "Well for a start your backswing seems to be much longer than normal and instead of accelerating the club down and through the shot, you appear to be slowing down and trying to scoop the ball up into the air."

My so-called friend was now warming to his task, so I quickly thanked him for his 'kind words' before he had the opportunity to totally destroy what little confidence I had left. What added to my sense of frustration was the fact that the rest of my game was reasonably good and at the next hole I once again hit a good tee shot. On most occasions I would have been delighted with my drive, but in this instance it had left me with exactly the kind of shot I did *not* want to play: a downwind pitch from around 100 yards, which also had to carry a bunker that guarded the front of the green.

Recalling my partner's analysis of my swing and being thoroughly fed up with either thinning or stubbing my wedge shots, I made up my mind to be as positive as I could about the next shot.

I had reached the stage when even hitting the ball clear over the green would have been preferable to the rubbish I had been playing.

Then it was the moment of truth. Head still, three quarter back swing, good shoulder turn, then it was weight back on

the left side, pulling the club down smoothly and accelerating through impact, making sure my head stayed down until the ball was well away.

Full of apprehension, I looked up eager to see the result of my efforts. Surely I had hit the shot too hard and the ball would fly over the green? Instead it pitched in front of the hole, took another bounce and then stopped dead, about ten feet past the flag.

"Nice shot," said my partner.

"Thanks, but I thought that second bounce was a bit hard," I replied, trying hard not to smile.

Try shortening your backswing (above) for more control on short iron shots.

One area of the game where the pros really excel is in the quality of their ball striking. This is reflected in the way they are able to stop the ball dead in its tracks, not just with the short clubs, but also with the long irons.

Now although getting a ball struck with a 3 iron to stop on the first bounce may be beyond the abilities of weekend golfers, there is no reason why we cannot sharpen up our ball striking with the medium and short irons.

Recently I re-discovered an old Gary Player practice drill that still works for me and which might also help those golfers who are currently hitting slightly behind the ball with the medium and short irons.

All it takes to brush up your ball striking is a piece of string, a few practice balls and half an hour on the practice ground. Lay the string in a straight line on the ground, place the ball just in front of, but touching, the string and then make your normal swing at the ball.

If you hit the ground fractionally behind the ball, then the clubhead will collect the string as it travels through the hitting area. If on the other hand you strike the ball correctly the club will contact the back of the ball first and then the turf, leaving the string still on the ground.

You may thin a few shots at first but once you gain confidence and are able to strike the ball first then turf, you should soon see a dramatic improvement in your ball striking. Then just watch those approach shots bite when they hit the green.

Placing a piece of string under the ball is a good aid to help you hit down into the ball.

A piece of string

Chipping

(Right) At address the hands are ahead of the ball and the weight is mainly on the left side.

(Opposite) The wrists break quickly in the backswing, taking the club up on a steep plane.

Chipping is one department of the game where a little practice can certainly pay dividends. Think about it. How many greens do you miss per round and how often do you get up and down in two when you do?

However, it is no good simply dropping a few balls on the edge of the putting green and chipping towards one of the holes. Although there may be times during a round when you will have a straightforward shot, more often than not, you will be faced with something a little more awkward, when you get out on the course.

In the case of the former, you can often get away with a less than perfect shot but when it comes to the latter and you find yourself up to the ankles in the heavy rough, there is very little margin for error.

Feet are so important when it comes to playing this type of shot. Will the ball shoot out low or high? Should you try to stab at it, or take a full swing? That's where the practice session pays off, and a few minutes spent in some heavy rough at the side of the practice ground will help answer those questions. Armed with the correct answers, you can attempt this type of recovery shot more confidently.

Consider a typical situation where the ball has just missed the putting surface, rolled down a fairly steep bank and come to rest in heavy rough but is still only a few yards from the pin. In this situation, the best club for the task is the sand wedge. This is because the heavy sole flange, coupled with the maximum loft, will combine to help the club cut through the rough and under the ball, getting it airborne as quickly as possible.

Most weekend golfers have problems with this type of shot because they tend to quit on it: chopping down into the grass behind the ball without attempting to swing the club through towards the target.

If you do not want to leave the ball still deep in the rough then you must adopt a positive attitude. Grip the club firmly enough to stop the grass from turning the face off line, but not so tightly that your hands and arms become so tense that you are unable to cock your wrists quickly in the backswing.

Your stance should be slightly open with the hands slightly ahead of the ball and the

face of the club laid a fraction open; a set-up position which is very similar to playing a bunker shot. With the ball positioned in the centre of your stance and the weight predominantly on your left side, break the wrists just after you start the backswing.

Try not to rush the downswing, but aim to build up speed smoothly, remembering to keep the left hand leading right through the impact. If you allow the right hand to overtake the left this will have the effect of reducing the loft on the face of the club

and it could result in the ball staying in the rough instead of popping up out of the rough and onto the grass.

Before you play the shot, try a few practice swings to get the feel for the shot and to also help judge the amount of resistance the club will have to overcome to get through the rough.

A word of warning. If you do have a few practice swings, make sure that you pick a spot well away from your ball. For if the ball moves as the result of your practice swing, it still counts as a shot.

(Left) The left hand leads through impact as the club drives down and through.
(Right) The head remains still as the club carries on through.

Thinning and skulling

There are few more frustrating things in golf than thinning or skulling a shot from just off the green: a problem that plagues most weekend golfers from time to time. It usually happens when we get a little anxious about stubbing the club into the turf behind the ball.

Instead of allowing the loft on the clubface to do its job, we either attempt to scoop the ball into the air by flicking at it with a loose, wristy action, or we lift our head too quickly, often before the club has even made contact with the ball.

The result of either of these faults is normally a shot in which the leading edge of the club makes contact with the centre of the ball instead of the bottom, producing a low, uncontrolled flight that sends the ball shooting across the green, turning what might have been a chip and putt par, into a bogey, or worse.

A less than sympathetic playing partner once claimed that he had a certain cure for golfers who lifted their head too soon when playing this type of shot. This cure comprised of a length of cord with a loop at one end and a fish hook at the other.

This loop was passed over the golfer's head and the fish hook positioned close to what I can only describe as a sensitive area of the anatomy. My partner assured me that if the golfer lifted his head, even fractionally, he would receive a painful reminder not to do so again!

Although I would hesitate to recommend that particular cure for skulling, lifting the head is certainly a major factor in a poor short game. A less painful method of keeping the head still, is to concentrate on watching the clubhead strike the back of the ball before looking up.

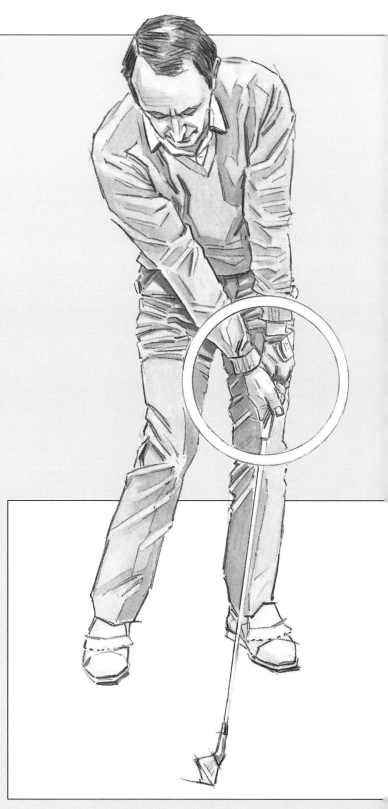

FROM TEE TO GREEN

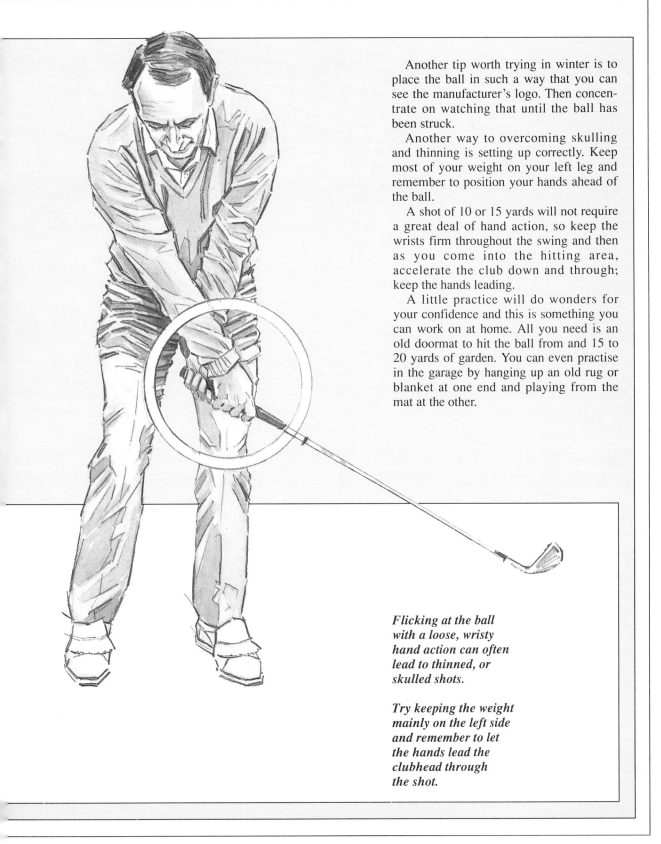

Another tip worth trying in winter is to place the ball in such a way that you can see the manufacturer's logo. Then concentrate on watching that until the ball has been struck.

Another way to overcoming skulling and thinning is setting up correctly. Keep most of your weight on your left leg and remember to position your hands ahead of the ball.

A shot of 10 or 15 yards will not require a great deal of hand action, so keep the wrists firm throughout the swing and then as you come into the hitting area, accelerate the club down and through; keep the hands leading.

A little practice will do wonders for your confidence and this is something you can work on at home. All you need is an old doormat to hit the ball from and 15 to 20 yards of garden. You can even practise in the garage by hanging up an old rug or blanket at one end and playing from the mat at the other.

Flicking at the ball with a loose, wristy hand action can often lead to thinned, or skulled shots.

Try keeping the weight mainly on the left side and remember to let the hands lead the clubhead through the shot.

AROUND THE GREEN

This is an area of the game where the top players really shine and that they practise more than any other because they know how many shots can be saved by getting close to the hole from just off the putting surface.

The main problems amateur golfers face playing the chip and run shot is stubbing the club into the ground behind the ball or alternatively catching the ball thin and skulling it through the green.

The first usually happens because the golfer makes a hurried stab at the ball, instead of allowing the clubhead to accelerate through towards the hole. The second fault can often be traced to the hands being behind, rather than in front of the ball, at the address position. Remember, you should be concentrating on keeping the hands ahead throughout the stroke and hitting forward and down, instead of trying to scoop the ball up into the air.

The club you choose depends on the type of shot you want to play. But if you are close to the green, with a straight forward line to the pin, it is easier to judge both distance and speed, by playing the

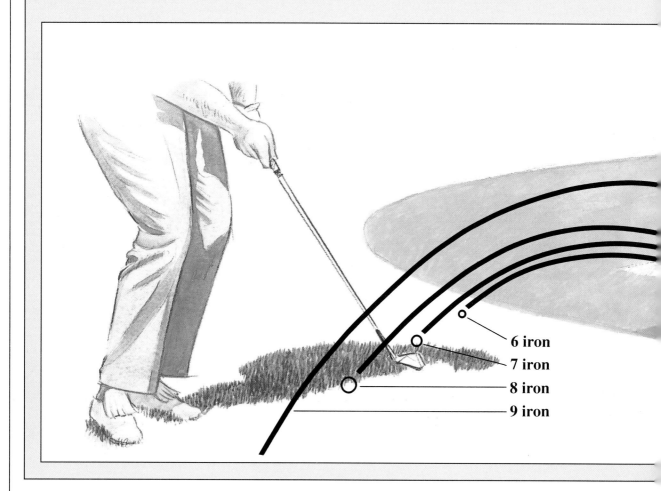

6 iron

7 iron

8 iron

9 iron

shot with a fairly straight faced club, such as a 5 or 6 iron, rather than a wedge.

The feet should be kept fairly close together, hands ahead of the ball with the head remaining absolutely still, until the ball has been struck. The weight is kept mainly on the left foot and the stance slightly open, to allow the hands and arms to swing through towards the target.

Once again, a smooth, slow tempo is vital and the only way to develop the right kind of feel for the chip and run shot is to spend a few minutes practising before you start to play.

Greenside

Depending on your position, you have the option to use several different clubs for chipping around the green. Your choice depends on how you see the shot, and also on the club with which you feel confident.

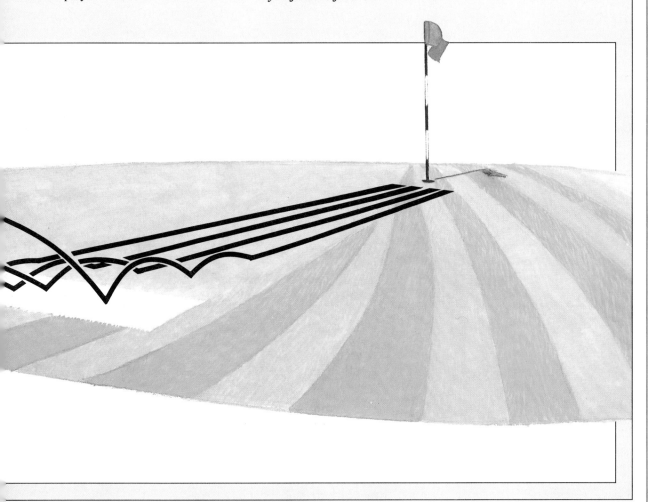

Divot check

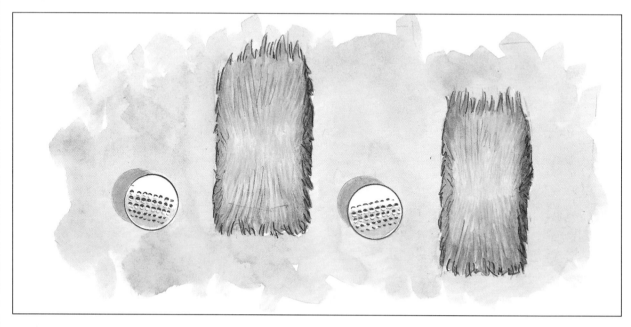

Something we weekend golfers admire about the pro game is the way the players can make the ball stop so quickly on the greens.

Believe it or not, square grooves aside, there is no secret to making the ball stop quickly, especially with the shorter irons. It is simply a matter of ensuring that the ball is struck first, before the club makes contact with the turf.

With the longer clubs like the driver and fairway woods, the length of the shafts dictate that the club is swung on a fairly shallow arc, or plane. This in turn means that sidespin has more effect on the flight of the ball than backspin; when was the last time that you saw someone get any backspin on a drive?

However, once you get to the shorter irons, the plane of the swing becomes more upright and backspin becomes the more dominant force; you might shank a wedge shot but you won't slice too.

You can swing the club as steeply as you like but unless the blade contacts the ball before the turf, the only way you will stop it quickly on the green, is to hit it directly into the hole!

Unfortunately, it is not easy to determine if you are striking the ball correctly. You know that if you have hit behind the ball when you hit a 'fat' shot but it becomes more difficult to establish if you are striking the ground just a fraction before the ball.

However, there is a method you can use to discover exactly where the club makes contact and all it requires is a couple of golf balls and a few minutes on the practice ground.

First, find a reasonably flat area of grass and then, using an 8 iron, hit a shot. Assuming you have taken a divot, place the next ball alongside the exact point where the blade of the club makes contact with the turf, or in other words, at the start of the divot mark. Then proceed to hit the second ball.

When you have played the shot, check if the impact point of the club lines up with the starting point of the previous divot. If they are in line then you have struck the ball before the turf. If on the other hand, the divot mark begins before the start of the first divot mark then the club has made contact with the ground before the ball.

To stop the ball quickly on the greens, check your divot. Place a second ball at the start of the divot mark. See if the club's impact point lines up with the starting point of the first divot.

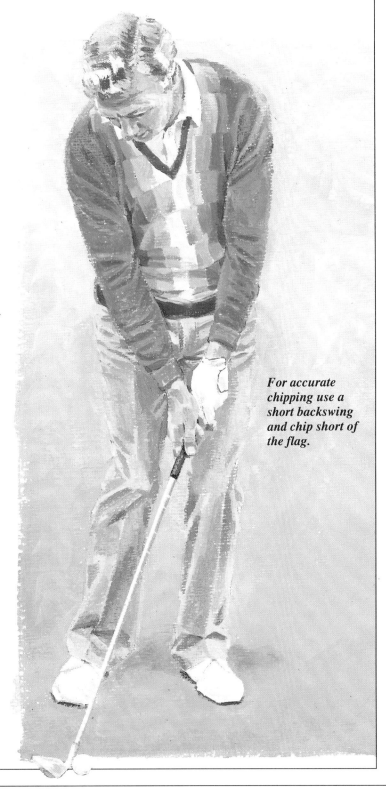

Lowdown on accuracy

More often than not, you will be best advised to chip your ball short of the flag because with a short backswing, you will not able to generate much backspin.

Look at the contours of the land to see where your ball will finish and how it will run on to the hole. Read the greens carefully for this feel shot.

This shot can be played with a straight-faced club although some golfers prefer to use a wedge and have their hands well forward of the club head.

It is essential to think positive with these shots and to visualize where the ball is going to land. As for all short shots around the green the swing does not reach more than waist height and it is essential to follow-through properly.

Tip from Brian Waites, professional at Hollinwell GC Notts, England.

For accurate chipping use a short backswing and chip short of the flag.

AROUND THE GREEN

Next time you are about to play a short iron approach shot, try to visualize the ball landing on the top of the flagstick.

Positive pitching

On the rare occasions that I have found myself in a good position to attack the pin, I have inevitably missed out by leaving my approach shots well short of the hole.

Anywhere on the green is usually good enough for me when hitting a fairway wood or long iron approach shot. Recently, however, I failed to cash in on a rare spell of straight driving from the tees that presented me with a fair number of short iron second shots.

To add to my frustration, I had been hitting these short irons quite well but I just could not get the ball up to the hole. Instead of putting for birdies, I more often than not found myself trying to get my first putt close enough to the hole to make sure I did not three putt!

I was actually beginning to dread hitting a decent drive, when I remembered some tips that I had received from a retired bank manager. From the tee, I would normally be a good 20 yards in front of him, but that never bothered my opponent, because he was a superb short iron player. Even on the long par 4 holes, where he was sometimes left with a third shot from as far away as 120 to 130 yards, he would inevitably put the ball close to the flag.

Eventually, he took me aside and revealed two pearls of pitching wisdom.

The first concerned the approach shot from around 120 yards where he claimed the secret of success was in taking one more club than you think you require, gripping slightly down the handle, and concentrating on rhythm instead of power. "If you are hitting the ball hard from this distance then you're hitting the wrong club" was the advice that I received. The problem with hitting the short irons hard is that we sometimes compact, or shorten the swing, to help control the force we put into the shot and the end result is usually a stab, rather than a swing.

So the next time that you find yourself within short iron range of the green try to resist the temptation to pull out the most lofted club you think you can reach the green with and hammering the ball as hard as you can. Instead, take one, or even two, clubs more than you think you need and play the shot with a smooth, full swing. Played correctly, this type of shot will give you much more control over the ball.

According to my tutor another reason why we are never up to the hole is because most weekend golfers subconsciously aim just to get the ball over the hazards, such as bunkers, which guard the green, rather than concentrating on hitting the ball up to the flagstick.

This stems from the fact that we amateurs never expect the ball to stop quickly when we play a shot to the green. Therefore, we tend to land the ball short and expect it to run to the hole. However, providing that the shot is played reasonably well there is no reason preventing us getting a short iron or wedge to stop pretty smartly on the green.

A good way to overcome the problem is to ensure that you select enough club for the required distance and then to aim to land the ball on the top of the flagstick, and not between the hole and the front edge of the green.

Finally, the next time you play, make a determined effort to hit the ball past the flagstick everytime you find yourself within short iron distance of the green. I am willing to bet that more than fifty per cent of your approach shots will still come up short of the hole, but at least you will have a few more putts for birdies, instead of three putting for bogeys.

Fluffed pitch shots

There are few more frustrating situations in golf than hitting two good shots just short of the putting surface on a long par 4 hole only to fluff that little chip shot to the green.

It is a shot that has let me down more often than I care to admit and one which led to me losing money, yet again, to an opponent several years my senior.

The golfer in question has never been a particularly long hitter, even as a young man, but he has always been something of a magician when it comes to getting up and down in two from just off the green. On this occasion, he was happy to pass on a couple of pointers, for the price of a pint.

The first tip was that unless you have to play the shot over a bunker or a mound in front of the green, leave the pitching wedge in your bag and reach for a middle iron. Then, instead of trying to lob the ball up into the air in the hope that it will carry just the correct distance before stopping close to the hole, try to visualize the shot as you would a long putt; the idea being to keep the ball low and allow it to run across the green towards the flag.

From close to the putting surface, the middle iron will provide enough loft to carry the ball over the fringe before landing on the edge of the green. And because there is less loft on the clubface, there will be less spin applied to the ball, making is easier to judge the length it will roll before stopping.

The second pointer concerned the grip and how changing it for this type of shot can help produce a more consistent strike and better results.

Instead of adopting your normal grip try using your putting grip for this shot. By doing so you will automatically firm up the wrists and help prevent topping or hitting behind the ball.

Set up with the knees flexed, stance slightly open and hands positioned ahead of the ball. Try to keep the hands ahead of

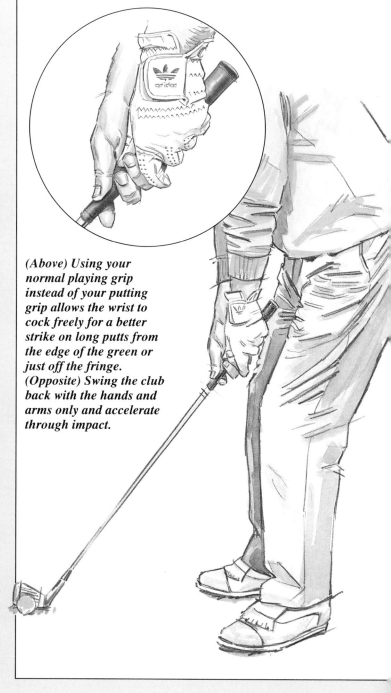

(Above) Using your normal playing grip instead of your putting grip allows the wrist to cock freely for a better strike on long putts from the edge of the green or just off the fringe.
(Opposite) Swing the club back with the hands and arms only and accelerate through impact.

the ball throughout the shot and perhaps most important of all, make sure that you accelerate the club in the through swing. This shot is played mainly with the hands and arms and very little leg or body action is required.

The length and pace of the swing is determined by the distance the ball has to travel; it therefore takes a little practice to build up some sort of muscle memory, for different lengths of shots.

Finally, once you are set up and ready to play the shot, forget the hole and concentrate instead on hitting the ball as close as possible to the spot on the green where you want it to land, before it starts to run towards the flag.

For the investment of a further half pint, I was able to glean another good tip to help get the ball close to the flag from just off the green but this time, instead of using a middle iron, the shot is actually played with a putter.

When you find yourself on the fringe of the green but a long way from the flag, the putter is the most reliable club to play. However, if you have to cover 20 or 30 yards, it means that you need a fairly long swing to generate enough clubhead speed to get the ball up to the hole.

With a shorter putt it is fairly easy to keep the wrists firm in the backswing but with a longer swing this becomes more difficult and can result in the ball being topped, or the putter head stubbing into the green behind the ball as it swings back and through towards the hole.

One way of avoiding this problem is to grip the clubhead as you would when playing a shot from the fairway instead of using a conventional putting grip.

This frees the wrists to cock more than they would normally when putting and makes it easier to produce a positive strike on the ball without having to swing the club a long way back in order to generate sufficient clubhead speed.

The perfect chip-and-run

The part of the game where most of we weekend golfers drop most shots is not driving; neither is it fairway woods or even bunker play. The sad fact is that we use up most of our handicap shots in the area between 10 and 15 yards from the green.

If you do not believe me, then next time you play in the monthly medal or a club stroke play competition, count the number of times you fail to get up and down in two from that area of approximately 10 to 15 yards from the putting surface. I do not have to tell you just how frustrating it can become watching shot after shot slip away; especially when you may just have hit two really good shots just short of the green on a long par four and then failed to make your par.

I have found myself in a similar situation on more occasions than I care to remember; no bunkers to carry or difficult slopes to negotiate, just a simple chip and run to get the ball close to the hole, leaving a tap in for par. Unfortunately, it seldom seems to work out that way. Instead it's usually a poorly played chip shot followed by a disheartening two putts and another shot has slipped away.

What adds to the sense of frustration is the fact that the shot does not really require a great deal of physical effort or a complicated technique in order to produce satisfactory results. It should, after all, be a

By standing close to the ball and gripping the club at the bottom of the handle, you will find it easier to swing the club along a straighter line to the target.

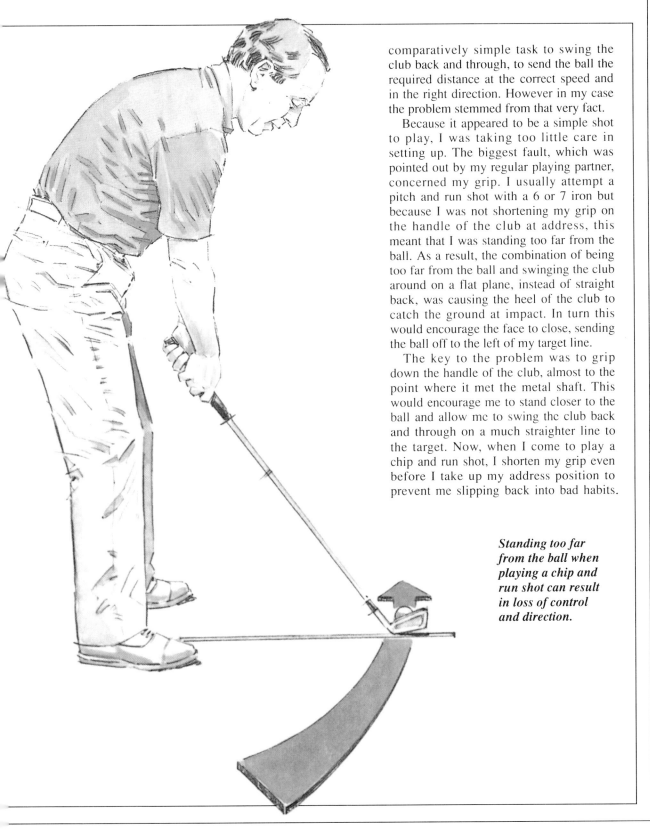

comparatively simple task to swing the club back and through, to send the ball the required distance at the correct speed and in the right direction. However in my case the problem stemmed from that very fact.

Because it appeared to be a simple shot to play, I was taking too little care in setting up. The biggest fault, which was pointed out by my regular playing partner, concerned my grip. I usually attempt a pitch and run shot with a 6 or 7 iron but because I was not shortening my grip on the handle of the club at address, this meant that I was standing too far from the ball. As a result, the combination of being too far from the ball and swinging the club around on a flat plane, instead of straight back, was causing the heel of the club to catch the ground at impact. In turn this would encourage the face to close, sending the ball off to the left of my target line.

The key to the problem was to grip down the handle of the club, almost to the point where it met the metal shaft. This would encourage me to stand closer to the ball and allow me to swing the club back and through on a much straighter line to the target. Now, when I come to play a chip and run shot, I shorten my grip even before I take up my address position to prevent me slipping back into bad habits.

Standing too far from the ball when playing a chip and run shot can result in loss of control and direction.

Sharpen up your short game

One of the best tips I ever received on the short game is to rely more on instinct, or feel, than on my technique.

On longer shots there is obviously more importance given to technique but on shots like the half wedge, the more target orientated you are, the better. It is rather like throwing a ball of paper into a waste-paper basket; you can 'hole out' time after time, until you start to think about how you are doing it!

Now this is all very easy to achieve in theory, but when it comes to putting it into practice out on the course, then it is a different matter. Nevertheless there are one or two points that you should concentrate on if you are really keen to sharpen up your short game.

At address, keep most of your weight on the left side because this encourages you to hit down on the ball. One problem high-handicappers suffer from is trying to scoop the ball up into the air; the outcome of this type of swing is normally to thin or top the shot. Just look at the amount of loft there is on a wedge. There is more than sufficient to get the ball well and truly airborne.

Because this type of shot only requires you to use your hands and arms, some people fall into the trap of mentally setting the rest of their body in concrete. All this does is stiffen up the other muscles and leads to poor shots. The legs should remain flexed and shoulders loose, but movements must be kept to a minimum.

Otherwise, it is basically the same set up as the one you would use when playing a full wedge shot, the ball towards the middle of the stance with the hands slightly ahead. We weekend golfers are often guilty of trying to steer the ball from close to the green, when in fact we would get much better results from trusting our natural instincts and allowing the club to swing freely.

The half wedge is simply a shortened version of the full wedge, so try to keep that feeling of smoothness uppermost in your mind as you swing the club. And remember, that just as you would follow through with a full wedge, then you should also keep the clubhead going on past impact with the half shot.

When it comes to those half wedge shots and short pitches, try to concentrate on feel and distance rather than technique. It is a little like lobbing balls of paper in a waste basket; you only start to miss when you begin to think about what you are doing.

CHAPTER SEVEN

Bunkers

The pitching wedge in bunkers

For most bunker shots the sand wedge is the ideal club for the job. Specifically designed to prevent the blade from digging too deeply into the sand behind the ball, the wide flange on the back of the sand wedge ensures that even we amateurs have a reasonable chance of getting out of trouble, provided that we follow the basic fundamentals of bunker play.

However, there are some occasions when we have to look at another club to get us out of trouble, especially when we find the ball plugged in the sand. When you find yourself facing this type of bunker shot then it is time to reach for the pitching wedge.

This is because in this instance, we require the club to penetrate deeply down through the sand instead of following the much shallower path that we would achieve when using a sand wedge. Because the pitching wedge does not have the wide flange at the back of the blade it can get down through the sand and virtually dig the ball out.

Unlike a normal bunker shot where the ball is sitting clearly on the surface, playing from a buried lie requires several adjustments to the address position and the swing technique.

Firstly, instead of setting up with the blade of the club positioned open to the target line, the pitching wedge must be positioned with the blade square to the target line. By setting the blade in this position it will help the club cut sharply down into the sand instead of bouncing through on a shallow arc.

You should also set up with the ball slightly further back in your stance than you would for a normal bunker shot. This will push your hands forward and encourage you to hit down and through the shot. Your stance should also be much squarer to the target than if you were playing a conventional bunker shot.

Obviously because you are hitting down more steeply on the ball your follow-through will be somewhat restricted. However, this does not mean you have to smash the ball as hard as you can just to get it out.

The final point to remember is that in playing this type of shot you will get no backswing on the ball whatsoever and it will come out of the bunker lower than a normal bunker shot.

(Opposite) Set up with the ball further back in your stance and the club face square or slightly closed.

(Below) The pitching wedge cuts down through the sand on a steep path, while the sand wedge (left) bounces through the sand on a much shallower path.

Greenside bunkers: weigh your options

One major difference between good golfers and weekend players such as myself, is that they tend to think before they play, whereas I all too often, play before I think.

This fault was perfectly illustrated when I partnered a low handicapper at my local club. When we reached the third hole, instead of missing the green on the right with my approach, which is my normal shot, I pulled the ball into the bunker to the left of the putting surface.

However, my pain was eased slightly when my playing partner also found the same bunker with his second shot, although I must confess he had a bad bounce just in front of the green. As I normally play from the other side of this particular green, when we reached the bunker I was surprised to find that it was remarkably shallow for a greenside bunker. As I was furthest from the hole and therefore first to play, I hauled out the sand wedge and set up to play my recovery

If your ball lands in a bunker, don't automatically reach for a sand wedge. Consider your options.

shot. The pin was about 10 feet from the bunker so I attempted to play a gentle splash shot that I hoped would pop the ball up out of the sand and send it rolling gently to the hole.

My backswing was nice and slow, but at the last minute I hurried the downswing through fear of leaving the ball in the sand, which of course, is exactly what I did! The next attempt did get the ball out but in making sure that I did not repeat my previous effort, I sent the ball to the far side of the green.

Feeling just a little annoyed, I watched with interest to see how a low handicapper would fare playing a similar shot and I couldn't believe my eyes when I saw he had a putter in his hands. I noticed that he had gripped down the handle and that he was careful to hold the head of the putter above the sand (if the head of the club had touched the sand as he addressed the ball he would have incurred a penalty shot) throughout the stroke which he appeared to hit only slightly harder than a stroke from a similar distance on the actual putting surface.

His swing appeared smooth and un-hurried and he seemed to catch the ball slightly on the upswing and the follow through looked a little exaggerated. The result was the ball came out as nice as you like and ran to within six inches of the pin, leaving him with a tap in par. Me? I three putted of course and dropped yet another shot to par.

The lesson to be learned is that when you land in a bunker don't just reach for your sand wedge. Take a few minutes to weigh-up your options, especially if the bunker has a shallow lip, the sand appears to be firm and the ball is lying cleanly.

Short memory

I was once having one of these rounds when every shot seemed to land in a bunker and the more bunker shots I had to play, the worse I played them. Throughout the first nine holes I continued to find the sand with unerring accuracy and my confidence was ebbing away with every shot. I felt that there was nothing dramatically different about the swing, but for some reason I seemed to be hitting into the sand too far behind the ball.

It was not until I was forced to play a bunker shot from a difficult lie that I realised what was wrong. On this particular bunker shot the ball had come to rest on an upslope at the side of the bunker, and as I set up to play the shot I went through my usual routine. Stance and shoulders slightly open, ball well forward and, finally, making sure that my feet were worked well down into the sand to establish a firm base from which to swing. On this occasion I also had to make allowance for the fact that the ball was well above my feet and therefore I gripped further down the handle to compensate.

It was then that the penny finally dropped. On all of my previous bunker shots I had forgotten that by working my feet well down into the sand, I had also lowered my body height. Therefore, because I had not gripped down the handle a few inches to compensate, it meant that the clubhead was making contact with the sand too far behind the ball, causing me to fluff the shot.

Unfortunately, finding the solution to my poor bunker shots did nothing to help me avoid the sand for the remainder of the round, but at least it allowed me to practise the cure.

If you're fluffing bunker shots, it may be that all you have to do is grip a few inches further down the handle.

CHAPTER EIGHT

The green

Concrete putts

Over the years I have learned that although the greens may be as hard as concrete that does not mean that they are as fast as lightning. In fact, when there is frost on the greens they can be much slower than normal conditions. This is because the frost, which tends to gather on the ball, slows it down as it rolls across the putting surface. Subsequently, as the frost melts the surface of the green becomes wet and this too will slow them down. And it is not until the greens dry out completely that they begin to pick up pace.

Frost and moisture on the greens can also have an effect on the amount that the ball will break. And a putt which might appear to break three or four inches will in fact move considerably less. Putts will also tend to stop much quicker in winter conditions and, in my personal experience, this usually happens when the ball is bang on line for the centre of the hole. So do not be afraid to give the ball a firm rap when there is a touch of early morning frost on the greens.

In some cases winter greens are brought into play when the frost is too severe and then your sense of humour will really be put to the test. Over the years I have tried all kinds of techniques to master winter greens, without any great success. In our winter fourball matches we have a gentlemen's agreement to concede any putt that is within the length of a putter grip from the hole. This not only prevents us developing a case of the yips, but also ensures that we remain friends!

One worthwhile tip that I picked up many years ago concerns how to get the best from your golf ball in cold conditions. When the temperature drops, the rubber in a golf ball becomes less resilient and the ball does not fly as far. One way to compensate for this problem is to carry an extra golf ball in your trouser pocket which your body heat will keep reasonably warm. You can then alternate that ball with the one you are using. I usually change golf balls every two holes providing of course that I can get that far without losing the balls.

On frosty greens putts will tend to break less than in normal conditions.

Putting into a target

Take a realistic view with long putts and aim to get the ball reasonably close to the pin.

When you find yourself a long way from the hole, resist the temptation to be over ambitious with your first putt. There is always an outside chance of holing a 60 footer, but all too frequently that 'never-up-never-in' approach leads to not one putt — but three. Far better to take a more realistic view and set your sights on getting the ball reasonably close to the hole.

One way to achieve that goal is to imagine that you are aiming to putt into a target area, six feet in diameter around the hole. Concentrate on keeping your head still and making a good solid contact with the ball, rather than attempting to find the exact line to the cup. There is no point in picking the right line if you leave the ball 10 feet short or knock it 15 feet past.

On the other hand, a properly struck putt, played at the right speed, even if not dead on line, should get you within that six foot target circle.

Practice putting:
Touch and feel

O nce about ten minutes before I was due to tee off in the monthly medal, I wandered over to the putting green. I had spent the previous half hour hitting practice balls and, to be honest, the experience had not left me exactly brimming over with confidence for the coming round.

It was not that I was hitting the ball all that badly. In fact I was striking it reasonably well; the problem was that I couldn't always be certain about the direction I was hitting it.

It was pretty busy when I arrived at the putting green, with golfers looking for that elusive touch with the putter which I can never seem to find until my card is history. It is only then that I start to hole putts. In they go from all over the green. Long, short, uphill, downhill, across the most vicious slopes, it makes no difference, the ball seems to be radar controlled.

I fished three reasonably round golf balls from my bag and looked for a hole that I could putt to. It was then that I noticed one of the older members who, despite his advancing years, was still considered to be one of the best putters in the club. I also observed that although there was one hole without anyone putting to it, our demon putter was ignoring the hole and appeared to be aimlessly rolling three balls across the green.

I watched a little more closely and noticed that often when he hit a putt, he would not even look up to see where the ball had gone. Occasionally he would adopt this practice with two, or even three, consecutive putts.

Curiosity, coupled with the hope that I might pick up a tip to help keep my medal card going for a few more holes than usual, prompted me to enquire into this peculiar putting practice. The old boy seemed genuinely pleased when I approached him and was only too glad to pass on what was the secret of his success on the greens.

Putting, he claimed, was ninety per cent confidence and ten per cent technique. And if, in my case, I had not been hitting the ball very well in my warm up session, my confidence wouldn't have been exactly bouyant before I went out to play.

Supposing I then carry on with my usual pre-round putting routine, which is to use three balls and attempt to hole all three every time. Now once again, assuming that my putting was on a par with my practice shots in terms of accuracy, by the time I had spent ten minutes missing putts, I might as well not bother to play in the medal at all.

Far better, my mentor believed, to putt without a target in mind. Instead, that ten minutes on the practice green would be far better spent concentrating on trying to establish a smooth stroke and targeting my full attention on striking the ball flush on the sweet spot of the putter every time. It was also a good idea to take note on just how far the ball rolls and to practise putting over upslopes, downslopes and across pronounced borrows. The key was to try to establish a feel for the pace of the greens rather than trying to hole each ball every time.

Touch and feel, the old boy reckoned, were the things which varied the most from day to day, not the putting stroke. And practising in this way, without any specific target in mind, does not dent your confidence in the way watching putt after putt slide by the hole does.

Concentrating on feel and pace on the practice green can pay dividends on the course.

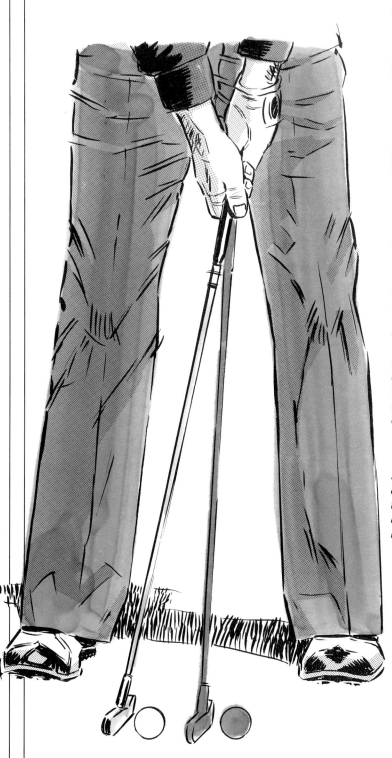

Trouble with medium and long range putts

I f you find that you are having difficulty in getting up to the hole on medium and long range putts, check that you do not have the ball positioned too far back in your stance.

If the ball is too far back, the hands may get ahead at address and this can lead to a downward strike on the ball that will produce backspin and cause the ball to stop quicker than you might anticipate.

If the ball is positioned further forward in the stance, with the hands above, or even slightly behind the ball, it is far more likely that the putter will strike the ball more on the upswing. This will impart overspin on the ball, making it run further.

Hands too far ahead and the ball is more likely to come up short on long range putts.

Fringe benefits

There are times when playing golf when you just can't help thinking "it's not my day". I was suffering one of those days the other week when every bounce was a bad one and every time that I missed the fairway I ended up with a dreadful lie.

Even when I eventually reached the greens, my problems were still not over. On no fewer than three different occasions, I found that approach shots which in the air, looked certain to land close to the pin, instead ran through to the back of the green and finished up sitting hard against the fringe.

As I said, my long putting has been bad enough without the complication of having to cope with this kind of problem. Even the pros have difficulty with this type of shot because it is impossible to ground the putter properly behind the ball. This often leads to the shot being topped and the ball coming up short or occasionally when hit a fraction too hard it can send the ball shooting well beyond the flag. Either way, playing this type of shot successfully is as much to do with luck as skill.

However, there is an alternative to using a putter when forced to play from against the fringe. It is a shot which the pros have perfected and one that might help you out of a tough spot. This particular shot is played with the sand wedge, or rather the leading edge of the sand wedge.

Set up to the shot by first of all holding the club well down the grip to ensure maximum control. Then, positioning the club just above the grass, line up the leading edge of the club with the middle of the ball. Holding the club at this height prevents the clubhead from snagging the grass in the backswing and also ensures a clean contact at impact.

Keeping the lower body very still and the wrists firm, swing the club back and through as if you were using your putter. Your aim should be to contact the ball on, or slightly about its equator, thus applying a touch of top spin to get it rolling just like a putt. This shot seems pretty complicated but is well worth taking time to learn if it will help you master one of the game's most frustrating shots.

There is an alternative to using a putter when playing from against the fringe. Take out a sand wedge and aim to strike the ball just above its equator for a touch of topspin to get the ball rolling just like a putt.

Single-handed success

An exercise that might help to improve your short and middle range putting is practising holding the club in your left hand only (in the case of left-handers the right).

Line up your putt as normal with both hands on the grip, but just before you start your stroke, take your right hand off the grip and put it either in your pocket or just let it hang freely by your side. Then go ahead and strike the putt as normal.

This simple training exercise might help you to ensure you keep the putter head acceleration on through the ball and also help prevent the right hand from taking over and turning the face of the putter to the left.

Once, during a particularly poor spell on the greens, in desperation I tried out this one-handed putting style for a complete round with remarkable results. I only three-putted once and holed almost everything from under six feet!

Putting single-handed helps to ensure the putter head accelerates on through the ball. Your short putting may improve.

I don't know about you, but short putts and bumpy winter greens are a combination that normally spells a lot of trouble.

While I appreciate that playing in winter means taking the rough with the smooth, nevertheless some greens, both proper and temporary, resemble the surface of the moon at this time of year. It doesn't seem to matter all that much with the longer putts because I don't really expect to hole a great many twenty footers, even on perfect putting surfaces in the middle of the season.

However, even in the depths of winter when I do get the ball to within three or four feet of the cup, it seems reasonable to expect to hole one or two.

My problem is being too tentative; I reason that as I'm only a few feet from the hole I shouldn't have to hit the ball too hard. But when I try to roll the ball gently towards the hole, it normally dribbles away to the left or right and even worse, often finishes up a foot short!

That was still my problem not long ago when I found myself playing on temporary greens. After my fourth three stab in six holes I was becoming just a little annoyed when one of my playing partners passed on a tip that had helped him get over the problem which was bugging me.

He suggested that when I was facing a three or four footer, I should try to imagine there was a tack sticking in the back of the ball and that I should attempt to tap the tack into the ball with a putter instead of making a tentative and stroking action.

By this time I was willing to try anything and to my amazement this method worked well for the rest of the round.

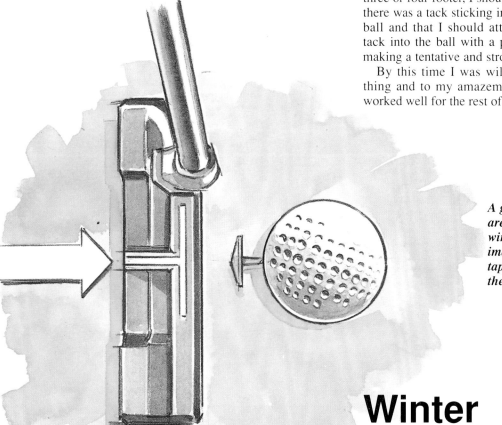

A good tip if you are tentative on winter greens is to imagine you are tapping a tack into the back of the ball.

Winter putting

The eyes have it

I find one of the most difficult aspects of putting is judging distance correctly, especially when it comes to putts around the 15 to 20 foot range.

I am not troubled by putts from outside that distance because I do not really expect to hole many. Instead, I tend to adopt the 'three foot circle' principle, whereby I concentrate on making a good smooth stroke while at the same time, trying to get the ball into an area which is within three feet of the hole. If the ball actually drops, then it is a bonus.

With short putts, unless there is a definite slope to contend with, I try to adopt a 'straight at the back of the cup' approach, at least, for as long as my nerve holds out!

However, when it comes to that middle distance I have often come a cropper trying to work out my priorities; should I concentrate on judgement of distance, as I do with long putts, or zero in on the hole, which is my method when it comes to short putts? On too many occasions the answer turned out to be neither. And there were many times when I still had not made up my mind while I was actually in the process of making the stroke!

The results, as you can imagine, were far from satisfactory. Therefore I was determined to work out the best method and then stick with it. The answer to the problem was eventually resolved, but as so often happens in golf, the solution came about by chance.

I had spent about an hour on the putting green trying out various ideas when one of my regular playing partners came over and we started to talk about a recent televized tournament. I had been practising with three balls and while we talked, continued to putt without really concentrating. When I looked up, to my surprise, all three balls were nestling close to the hole.

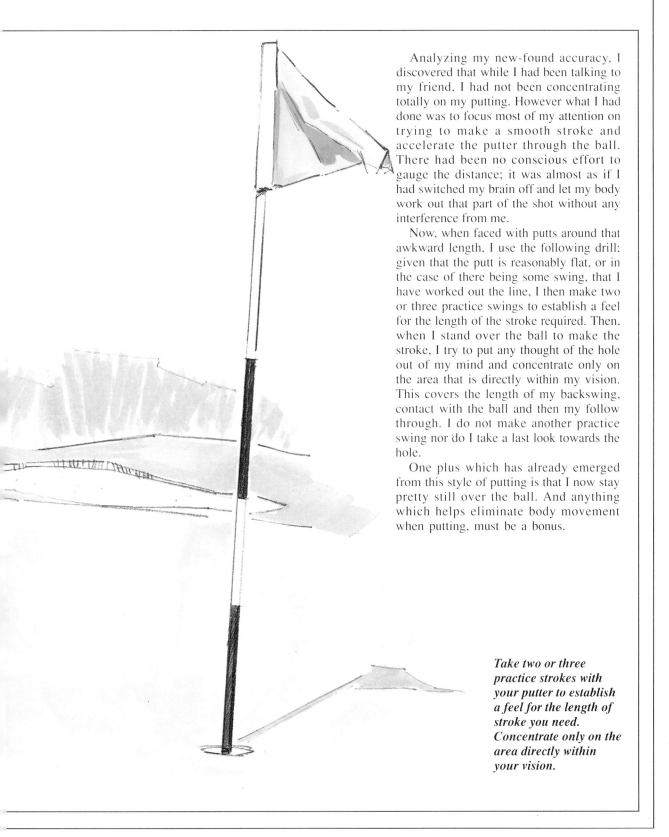

Analyzing my new-found accuracy, I discovered that while I had been talking to my friend, I had not been concentrating totally on my putting. However what I had done was to focus most of my attention on trying to make a smooth stroke and accelerate the putter through the ball. There had been no conscious effort to gauge the distance; it was almost as if I had switched my brain off and let my body work out that part of the shot without any interference from me.

Now, when faced with putts around that awkward length, I use the following drill; given that the putt is reasonably flat, or in the case of there being some swing, that I have worked out the line, I then make two or three practice swings to establish a feel for the length of the stroke required. Then, when I stand over the ball to make the stroke, I try to put any thought of the hole out of my mind and concentrate only on the area that is directly within my vision. This covers the length of my backswing, contact with the ball and then my follow through. I do not make another practice swing nor do I take a last look towards the hole.

One plus which has already emerged from this style of putting is that I now stay pretty still over the ball. And anything which helps eliminate body movement when putting, must be a bonus.

Take two or three practice strokes with your putter to establish a feel for the length of stroke you need. Concentrate only on the area directly within your vision.

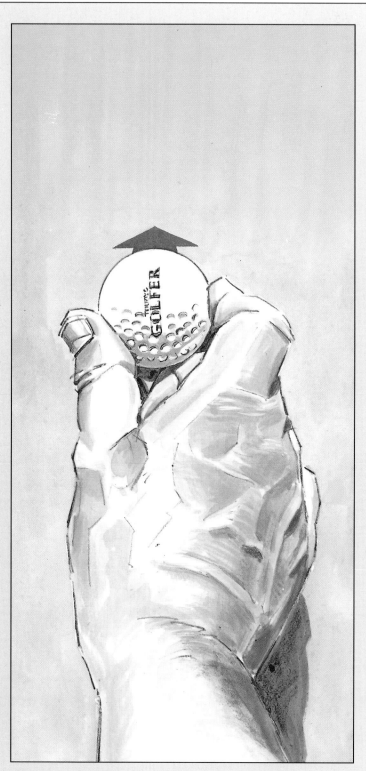

Lining up the manufacturer's golf ball logo is an invaluable putting aid.

Using the maker's name and logo

No doubt you will have noticed how much care the pros take when it comes to marking their ball on the green but have you ever been aware of why some of them seem to take even more care when they replace it?

In most instances, the reason for all this care and attention is to help them to establish the correct line for their putt. When they replace the ball, some players like to use the maker's name and logo as a pointer. They position the lettering on the ball in a direct line, either towards the hole or in the case of a putt with some break on it, along the line they want to start the ball off on.

They are not infringing the rules in any way and some of the top pros swear by this method of lining up putts because they feel that by stroking the ball along the line of the lettering printed on the ball, they can produce a more accurate strike and hopefully hole more putts.

Judging the pace of a putt

Being able to judge the speed of a putt is really more important than being able to read the line perfectly, especially if you are a long way from the hole.

However, you can learn something about the pace of your putt simply by studying the putting surface itself. When the greenkeeper cuts the green the mower leaves a striped pattern on the surface. The darker strip is where the mower has cut against the natural grain of the grass and the lighter strip is the result of cutting with the grain.

This means that the grass in the darker strip will be standing more upright and therefore it will provide more resistance to the ball running over it. On the other hand the grass in the lighter strip is lying flatter and this will allow the ball to run with less resistance, producing a faster putt.

With the grain the putt will run faster. Putting against it will call for a firmer strike.

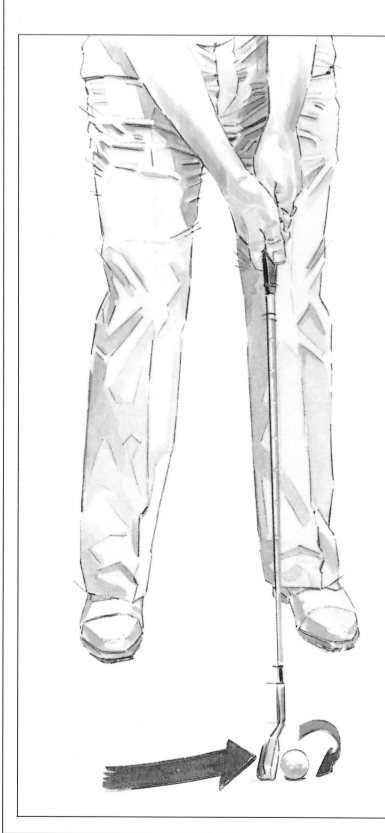

Get your putting on the up

O ne of the most exasperating feelings in golf is to hit a putt dead on line, watch it follow the borrow as if guided by laser, turn perfectly towards the cup, and then stop six inches short of the hole!

And when this happens to you not just once, but on four or five occasions during a single round you might be forgiven for asking, "Why me?" But before you sling your putter into the nearest lake or condemn it to the darkest corner of the attic, it might just be worth checking out something in your set-up that might be the cause of your frustration.

In my case, I was trying out my fourth putter in as many weeks, when it was suggested to me that I might have the ball too far back in my stance. I must confess that initially I was not too keen on making any alterations because I felt that I was getting the putts on line and that the problem was simply not hitting the ball firmly enough. However, my putts were still finishing short of the hole even when I felt that I had hit the ball firmly enough to go a foot or so past the cup, and it was then that I recalled a tip many years ago from a gentleman by the name of Harold Swash who had designed putters for several of the leading club manufacturers.

Harold had demonstrated to me the difference in distance which occurs between two putts, each struck with similar strength, when one ball is hit with the putter moving slightly on the downswing and the other when the club is travelling on the upswing. In the case of the ball struck on the downswing, a certain amount

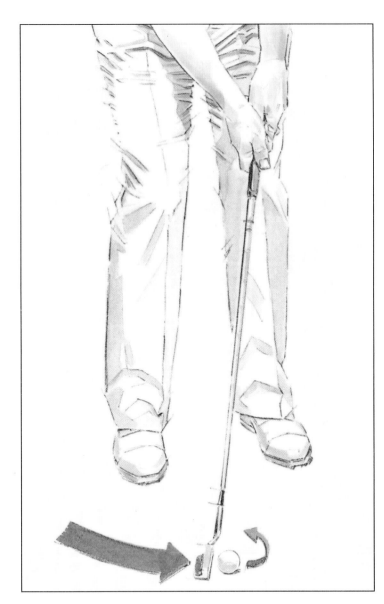

of backswing is imparted on the ball, with the result that it will sometimes actually check, or skid slightly, before it begins to roll, and as a result, will not travel as far as you might anticipate.

However, in the case of the ball that is struck slightly on the upswing, overspin is created and the ball tends to run a little more smoothly and subsequently travels further.

Because I had the ball positioned towards the middle of my stance, I discovered that I was striking down on it slightly and creating that drag factor which resulted in the ball not travelling as far as I anticipated. By moving the ball more towards my left foot, I was able (without changing my stroke) to strike the ball when the putter head was travelling slightly on the upswing, which helped the ball roll more smoothly and travel the correct distance.

(Left) Hitting the ball slightly on the downswing with the putter can sometimes result in putts coming up short.

(Opposite) Striking the ball slightly on the upswing can help to get it rolling more smoothly.

On-line putting

When it comes to judging the correct amount of break on a putt, to my surprise, I find that I am usually not all that far out. However, when it comes to directing the ball along the correct line, it is a different story.

I am usually a little more successful with left-to-right putts than with right-to-left efforts. And although I still do not hole anything like the number I should, I take comfort from the fact that the majority of my efforts miss on the high, or 'pro' side of the hole.

Why this should be and why I am better with breaks from one side rather than the other, had always been a mystery to me until one day I literally stumbled on a possible reason.

Playing in a match, I pulled my approach shot to the left and from my position down the fairway, it looked odds on that the ball would finish in a greenside bunker. However when I arrived on the green, I discovered that the ball was still above ground — but only just. Instead of running into the bunker, the ball had stopped a foot or so short of the sand.

I was busily congratulating myself on my good fortune until I realised that it was going to prove just a little difficult to take

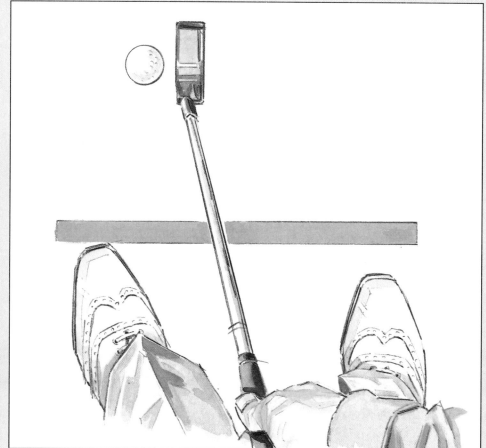

Putting with a slightly closed stance has helped me get the ball started on the correct line with left-to right putts.

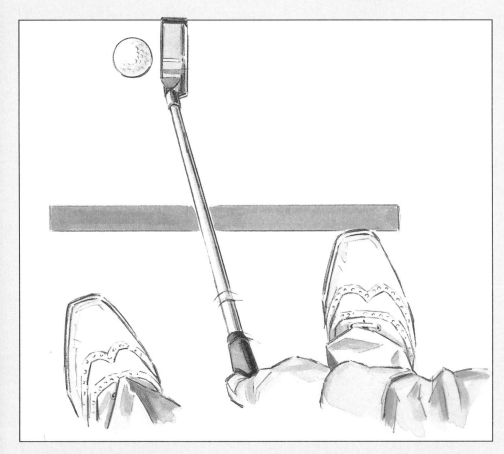

An open stance on right-to-left putts has allowed me to push the putter through on the right line.

up a proper stance. That was, if I intended to hit the ball in the general direction of the hole. My first attempt at addressing the ball almost sent me toppling into the bunker and I had to stop for a moment and think out a better alternative.

My normal stance is slightly closed, with the ball positioned just inside my left toe, but there was no way I could take up that position in this instance. To get both feet on the putting surface meant that I was forced to adopt a slightly exaggerated, open stance. The putt I was facing was around 20 feet, with a pronounced right-to-left borrow, so I was not brimming over with confidence. However, to my surprise on this occasion I actually managed to get the ball rolling along the line that I had picked and although I did not manage to hole the putt, it went close enough to send me toppling over into the bunker in

excited anticipation, a fraction of a second before the ball rolled just past the right lip.

A few holes later I was facing another right-to-left putt and recalling my enforced open stance, I tried a less exaggerated variation and to my delight, and the disbelief of my playing partner, the ball ran perfectly on line and dropped into the hole for my only birdie of the day. Walking to the next tee he claimed that it was at least a 40 footer but modesty demands that I set the record straight; it was only a 35 footer.

Throughout the remainder of the round I used my new putting method; adopting an open stance for the right-to-left putts and staying with my normal slightly closed set-up for the left to right efforts. And although I by no means holed everything in sight during the remaining holes, I did sink a few and those missed were through either mis-reading the line or pace.

The spot-putting technique

If you find it difficult to get the ball close to the hole when faced with a putt across a sloping green, try adopting the 'spot putting technique'.

Once you have assessed how much your ball will break, say for example two feet, then look for a spot to aim for which is two feet to the left or right depending on the angle of the slope.

And then forget the hole and aim your putt straight at the spot you have picked out. That spot can be a mark on the green or tree or bush behind the green, just so long as whatever you choose acts as a sighter for your putt.

However, if you find difficulty picking a suitable spot close to the hole, especially when it comes to long putts, then choose a point three or four feet along your intended target line instead.

How much you think the putt will break will determine the amount of borrow you will have to play. The thought to keep in mind is that you would like the ball to travel from your putter face directly towards the spot that you have picked and then as it loses pace it should start to curve down towards the hole.

Pick your spot and try to hit your putt straight towards it.

Getting back on the right path

This tip emerged as the result of a lunch-time putting contest in the office, the winner of which modesty forbids me to name.

However, during the course of the contest, the conversation, as you might expect, centred around various putting styles and techniques, including how difficult it was to be sure that you were taking the putter straight back and through especially on these testing five and six footers.

It was during this discussion that I remembered a tip I received many years ago in a Pro-Am after a particularly disastrous day with the putter, during which I missed at least half a dozen putts from that range; pushing the ball to the right on each occasion.

The problem with putting, as with all the other aspects of the swing, is not so much what you are actually doing, but what you think you are doing. In my case, I was convinced that I was taking the putter back in a straight line and that I was also holding the face of the club square to the target right through the stroke (if you could call it that).

What I was actually doing, was fanning the club open in the backswing as the result of taking the club back too much on the inside. Then when I struck the ball, instead of the face being square, it was open and that's why I kept missing the hole on the right.

The professional in our team, suggested that I try the following exercise to help illustrate what I was in fact doing and secondly, to get me back on the right path once I had realised the errors of my ways.

He told me to take my normal putting stance with the toe of the putter as close as

possible to the skirting board that runs along the bottom of a wall. Then, simply swing the putter back and forth, for the appropriate distance required.

Because I had the wall as a reference to what was actually square, the deviation in line immediately became apparent.

If you are pushing the ball to the right of the hole on short putts, you may be fanning the club open in the backswing.

Stand up to your putts

There are few more annoying experiences in our golf than continually missing short putts, and I have experienced more than my fair share of them.

It always seems that just when I am beginning to get the other parts of my game working reasonably well, my putting starts to let me down.

On this occasion it wasn't my approach putting which was the culprit; the fault was failing to hole short putts with any degree of consistency. And it wasn't as if I was missing the hole on the same side every time; I would be just as likely to pull the putt as push it.

Frustration prompted me to think about buying another putter, but the Scot in me was loath to part with the money, unless it was guaranteed to cure my problems. While I was contemplating the situation, I idly picked up a putter belonging to one of my regular playing partners. By sheer coincidence, the player concerned happened to be one of the best putters in the club, but looking at this putter it was difficult to see why. It was at least twenty years old and the shaft was rusty.

One other thing that I noticed was how thick the grip was in comparison to my own putter. I took a couple of golf balls from my bag and hit a few putts with this rusty old relic. There was not a great deal of difference with the long putts but I was pleasantly surprised at how many of those three footers that I had been missing started to drop.

Returning the putter to its owner I asked him if his putter had that thick grip when he first acquired it. "No," he replied. "It had a fairly thick grip, but after I bought it I started to miss too many short putts and decided to have a lesson with the pro."

It seems the pro reckoned my friend's hands were too active in the stroke and this was the reason he was missing those short putts. The pro went on to suggest that one of the best cures for this problem was to put a thicker grip on the putter.

This, he claimed, would have the effect of limiting the hand action and transferring the putting action to more of an arms and shoulder movement.

"Did it work?" I asked. "Well,' he replied, "I've had this putter for almost twenty years and the only thing I ever changed about it, was the grip."

I headed for the pro shop with new hope and a happy heart. For not only had I discovered the answer to my putting problem; the cure looked like working out a lot cheaper than I had first thought.

Another tip which you might find helpful if you are experiencing problems keeping your short putts on line is to stand more erect at address.

Standing more upright on short putts will move you closer to the ball. This will also make it easier to take the putter back in a straight line.

If you stand too far away from the ball, it can encourage you to take the putter back more in an arc than a straight line. This can lead to pulling the ball left or pushing it right of the hole at impact.

Try to get your eyes over the ball in the putting stroke by standing taller to the ball. This will enable you to take the putter back on a straighter line.

Seaside greens

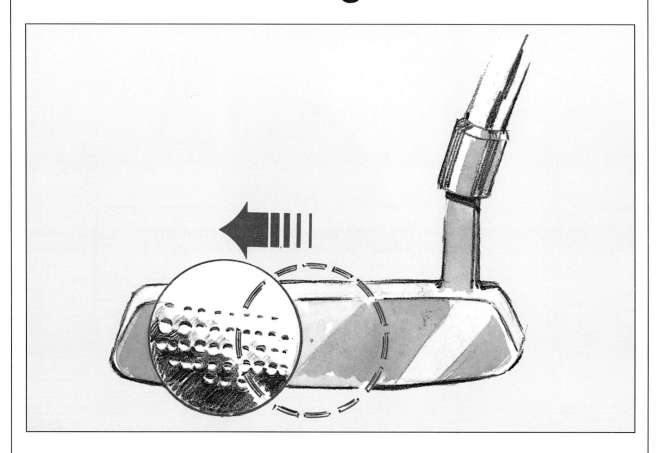

Personally, I enjoy putting on seaside greens. They are in the main, about the same pace and with a few notable exceptions, reasonably flat.

The putting surface on links courses can often be very large; the Old Course at St Andrews for example, has greens which cover an area of several acres!

When it comes to putting on large greens you should concentrate on simply trying to get close to the hole; concentrate on the pace, rather than trying to read every little borrow.

If, on the other hand, you should find yourself on a contoured green, facing a slippery downhill putt, it can be extremely difficult to stop the ball close to the hole. In this situation, there is a tendency to try to dribble the ball down the slope in the

hope that it might just reach the cup. However that type of stroke does not create the proper rolling action and the ball is much more likely to run off line; or worse still, stop well short of the hole, leaving a tricky two or three footer.

One way that might help you overcome the problem of striking the ball firmly enough to get it rolling properly, without charging ten feet past, is to address the putt with the ball positioned, not at the sweet spot in the centre of the blade, but instead slightly towards the toe of the club.

This has the effect of deadening the impact, thus allowing a more positive strike to help keep the ball on line.

On seaside greens the putting surface can be tricky, so concentrate more on the pace rather than the borrow.

CHAPTER NINE

Playing in difficult weather

Chipping

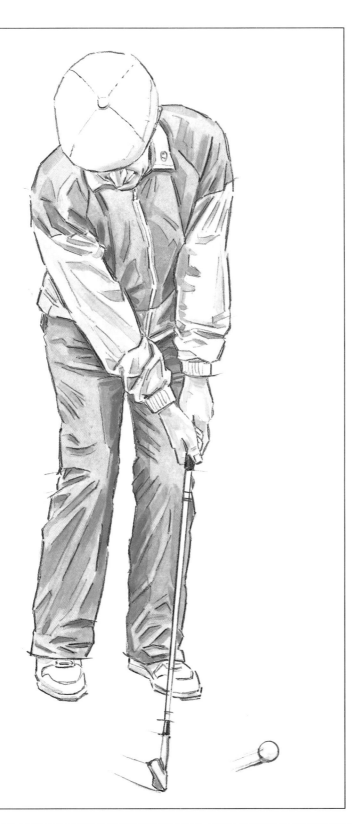

T rying to get the ball close to the hole from within a few yards of the edge of a temporary green is one aspect of winter golf that would test the patience of a saint.

Personally, I always feel that the ball will run much faster across the surface than it actually does, with the result that I inevitably try to be too precise with my chip, stub the club, normally a wedge, into the ground behind the ball and you can guess the rest.

Once however, while playing in a local office tournament, I decided to leave the wedge in the bag for this type of shot and instead, used a combination of my putting action and an 8 iron. I ended up with the 8 by a process of elimination after trying, first of all my putter, then my 9 iron, both of which produced erratic results.

The 8 iron seemed to work best because, although it got the ball up in the air, the flight was shallow enough for the ball to roll a reasonable distance on landing. This seemed to help me get the ball closer to the flag than with any of the other clubs.

In fact, I went so far as to use my orthodox putting grip when playing the shot but I made sure that my hands remained ahead of the clubface throughout the swing, which is simply back and through, with no wrist action.

Obviously, we all want to play our very best every time we tee the ball up, but at the end of the day, I suspect most winter golfers, myself included, are happy just to have the opportunity to play, if and when the weather permits.

With that thought in mind, the next time you catch a glimpse of watery winter sun, and take the opportunity to play a few holes, you might find one or two of these tips will help you get a little more enjoyment from your winter golf.

Using an 8 iron and my putting grip, I keep my wrists firm and try to keep the club low, both in the backswing and the follow through.

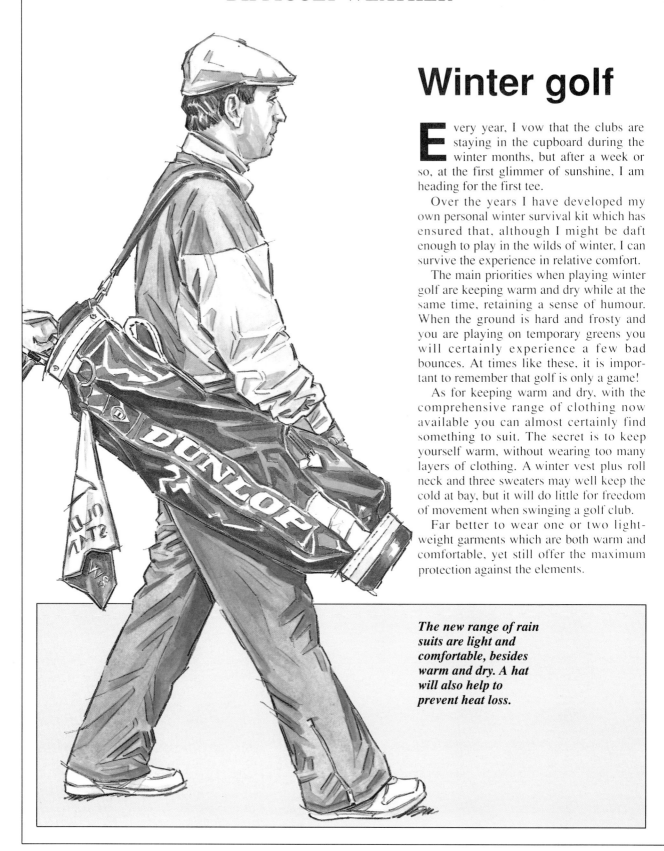

Winter golf

Every year, I vow that the clubs are staying in the cupboard during the winter months, but after a week or so, at the first glimmer of sunshine, I am heading for the first tee.

Over the years I have developed my own personal winter survival kit which has ensured that, although I might be daft enough to play in the wilds of winter, I can survive the experience in relative comfort.

The main priorities when playing winter golf are keeping warm and dry while at the same time, retaining a sense of humour. When the ground is hard and frosty and you are playing on temporary greens you will certainly experience a few bad bounces. At times like these, it is important to remember that golf is only a game!

As for keeping warm and dry, with the comprehensive range of clothing now available you can almost certainly find something to suit. The secret is to keep yourself warm, without wearing too many layers of clothing. A winter vest plus roll neck and three sweaters may well keep the cold at bay, but it will do little for freedom of movement when swinging a golf club.

Far better to wear one or two lightweight garments which are both warm and comfortable, yet still offer the maximum protection against the elements.

The new range of rain suits are light and comfortable, besides warm and dry. A hat will also help to prevent heat loss.

Beat the wet with woods

Winter inevitably brings wet as well as cold and there will be many occasions when the fairways will be damp and soggy. With this in mind, when it comes to playing long shots from the fairway, try using a fairway wood instead of an iron. The reason being, that when you play a long iron in wet conditions, water tends to get between the ball and the face of the club and this has the effect of reducing the amount of spin imparted on the ball.

Because it is spinning less, the ball will not get airborne as easily as in the dry and a less than perfect strike might not even get into the air at all. With a fairway wood, the swing is more of a 'sweeping' action and this makes it easier to get the ball up and away.

In wet conditions it is easier to get the ball airborne with a fairway wood, than a long iron.

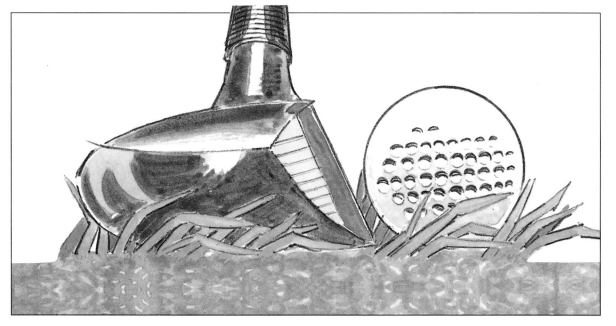

Hot teas and thermals

Many golfers now wear thermal underwear when playing in winter and many of the sets currently on the market are first class; offering both comfort and warmth, without feeling as if you are in a mobile sauna bath. Thanks to advances in technology, the manufacturers can now produce materials that allow the body to breathe, thereby preventing moisture forming inside the garment.

My one winter golf luxury is a cashmere roll neck sweater which I acquired at a sale in the famous Woollen Mill that stands beside the 18th fairway at the Old Course in St Andrews.

Even at the sale price, it was not exactly cheap but it does the job of two ordinary sweaters, providing warmth without bulk.

However perhaps the greatest boon in recent years to winter golf, has been the development of a new range of rain suits; most of which not only keep the golfer warm and dry, but are so light and comfortable to wear, that you are hardly conscious that you have them on at all. Their other advantage is they are roomy and do not greatly restrict your swing.

On the accessories side, the main priorities are (if you will pardon the term) the body's extremities. Twenty per cent of body heat can be lost through the head, therefore a hat of some description is the best method of preventing major heat loss. Some golfers prefer to wear the traditional style cap while others use ski-type woollen hats which have the added advantage of covering the ears. A pair of good quality golf socks are also essential.

You must also ensure that your hands are protected from the cold. When your hands get cold you begin to lose feel in your fingers and your game will undoubtedly suffer as a result. With this in mind, it is worth investing in a pair of mittens which you can wear between shots and which will certainly keep your hands warm, even on the coldest days.

I know that in winter many golfers carry a hip flask and that the odd tot of whisky, rum or brandy is said to help keep you fortified against the cold. Unfortunately, although spirits will certainly warm you up, the effect is short lived and the alcohol contributes little to long term warmth.

Far better to carry a flask of hot tea or coffee which can then be sparingly laced with your favourite tipple, just to enhance the flavour, of course!

As far as equipment is concerned, I have always used the winter time for experimenting; trying out new clubs and working on different parts of my game that may have given me trouble over the previous year.

I choose this time of year for two reasons. Firstly, if I am going to change say, my woods, or try out a new wedge, I can do so without there being any pressure on my swing. Secondly I do not expect the course to be at its best and therefore do not expect too much of my game at this time of year. If I decide to try a new set of clubs, it gives me enough time to get used to them before the season gets properly underway in the Spring.

An exercise which you may find helpful is to use only half a set of clubs while playing in the winter. One week leave out the odd numbered clubs; the next the even. This not only makes the bag lighter to carry but also gives me the opportunity to practise more half shots and work on acquiring a better feel for different types of shot that I have to play to compensate for the missing clubs.

The less sweaters you wear, the easier it is to swing the club, but not everyone can afford a new suit or cashmere sweater even at sale prices. That being the case, if you do have to wear one or two extra layers of

If you feel your swing is restricted by wearing winter clothing, try using a three-quarter swing and take one more club than normal.

FROM TEE TO GREEN

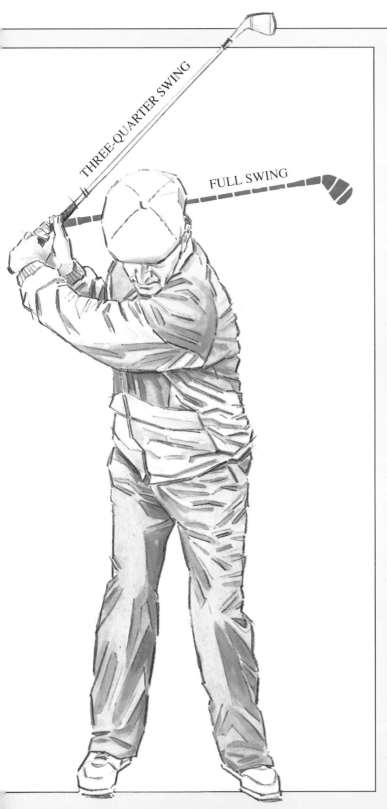

THREE-QUARTER SWING

FULL SWING

clothing while playing winter golf, remember that this can restrict your ability to make a full shoulder turn.

This is something that you should remember when it comes to club selection. And if you feel that the best you can achieve is a three-quarter swing, then take one club more than normal to compensate.

With a fairway wood, the swing is more of a 'sweeping' action and this, combined with the heavier head of the wood, makes it easier to get the ball up and away.

The type of golf ball you use can also make a difference to your play in the winter months. It is a common belief that the solid ball is best in winter months, although there are occasions when you might get a better result playing a wound ball.

When the weather is wet, you want the ball to fly as far as possible simply because it gets virtually no run when it lands. With the advances in dimple design and aerodynamics that have now been incorporated into many of the wound balls currently on the market, you might discover that you can fly this type of ball further than a solid one.

However, in cold weather it is advisable, even when playing a wound ball, to pick one with a Surlyn, rather than a Balata cover. This is because Surlyn reacts better in the cold than Balata.

When the ground is like concrete and there is a heavy frost, I always make sure that I have a sturdy pitch mark repairer in my pocket. I carry this implement not so much for repairing pitch marks, which are virtually non-existent in these conditions, but instead to chip away at the ice that forms around the spikes on my golf shoes. This build up of ice can make it difficult to keep your balance, especially when hitting a full shot. Therefore, it is a good idea to clear the ice away with the pitch mark repairer before you tee-off at each hole, or until such time as the sun melts the frost on the fairways and greens.

DIFFICULT WEATHER

(1)

(2)

(3)

Beat the breeze

After battling through the cold and wet of the winter months, we also have to cope with some strong winds in spring.

Having learned my golf on seaside courses, I discovered at an early age that one of the keys to playing well in windy conditions is good balance. When you are being buffeted by a gale, it can be almost impossible to keep your swing slow and smooth, nevertheless there are a couple of tips which might help you keep your feet on the ground!

The easiest way to improve your balance in the wind is to adopt a wider stance. This will certainly provide a firmer platform from which to swing the club but

FROM TEE TO GREEN

(1) Always take at least one club more when playing into a strong headwind.

(2) Gripping the club further down the handle will give you more control in the wind but will result in a loss of distance. Remember to take an extra club to compensate.

(3) A wider stance will help you keep your balance better in the wind but this will also restrict your turn. Go up a club to compensate.

there is a price to pay. The wider your stance, the more difficult it becomes to make a full turn, and as a result you will probably be at least a club shorter in distance than you would be under normal conditions.

The answer is not to try and hit the ball harder! Instead, take one, or even two clubs more than the distance would indicate and try to swing smoothly. Ideally, you should try to practise this shot before going out to play, in order to build up both your confidence and feel for the pace and rhythm required for this type of shot even in calm weather, something that I have found to be a great help when I have experienced problems with my timing.

Another tip which might help you play better in the wind is to grip further down the handle of the club than normal. The closer to the ball you are, the more control you will have over your shots. Once again, there is a price to pay in distance for this extra control. So when it comes to playing approach shots, remember once again to take one club more to compensate for gripping further down the handle.

The theory which I normally adopt when playing in a headwind is: take one club extra for the wind, one more for gripping down the handle, and if the wind is exceptionally strong, add a third, for taking up a wider stance.

Driving into the wind

When it comes to driving into the wind, you might think the logical approach would be to tee the ball lower than normal in the belief that this will help the ball fly under the wind. However, it does not quite work out like that.

When the ball is teed too low, there is a tendency to hit down on it which results in backspin being imparted on the ball. This causes it to rise far too quickly, which is the last thing you want to happen, playing a long par 4 into the wind.

When you get the chance to play downwind, resist the temptation to try to simply smash the ball out of sight. This is because regardless of how strong the following wind, if you rush the shot, striving for distance, the chances are you will misshit it and any advantage that might have been gained from the following wind, will have been wasted.

There are also times when you would be better served by hitting a 3 wood, rather than the driver, on a downwind hole. Firstly because the 3 wood is an easier club to control than the driver, and secondly, by getting the ball well up in the air, you can gain the maximum advantage from the following wind.

There are two easy methods of improving your control in blustery conditions. The first concerns the way in which you grip the club and the second concerns your stance.

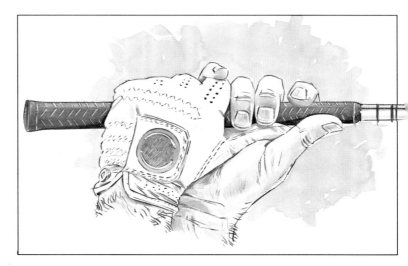

When the wind blows it is difficult to gain good balance and therefore it becomes much harder to control your swing. When this happens you can end up hitting shots off line and if you happen to be playing the driver, then there is a fair chance you might never see the ball again!

To help give you more control, try gripping further down the handle than you would in normal conditions. By doing so you will automatically bring yourself closer to the ball at address, which in turn, will help make your swing that little more compact and help provide extra control.

Another aid to better balance when the wind is blowing and one which applies to both shots from the fairway and the tee, is

To give yourself more control in windy conditions try gripping further down the handle. This will bring you closer to the ball at address and help make your swing more compact.

Teeing the ball too low into the wind can cause you to chop down on it at impact instead of sweeping it away with the full face of the club.

FROM TEE TO GREEN

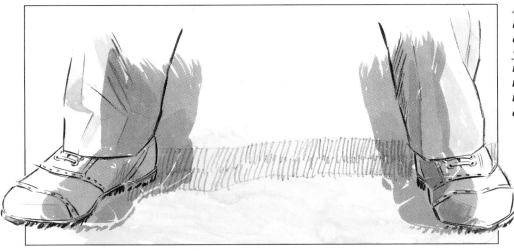

Another aid to better balance in blustery conditions is to widen your stance. This will restrict your shoulder turn so you may have to use more hand action in the shot.

to widen your stance. However, a word of warning: although this will provide a more solid base from which to swing, it will also restrict the amount of turn you will be able to make. In order to compensate for this reduction in shoulder turn you may find it necessary to use slightly more hand action than normal. This is a point which is well worth reminding yourself of just prior to starting your swing. Also, make an effort to employ as full a shoulder turn as possible, without losing your balance.

When playing a long par 3 in a strong crosswind, don't simply aim further left to compensate for the wind direction, as this can result in a destructive slice. Instead, try to hit the ball at a specific target then let the wind bring it back on the right course.

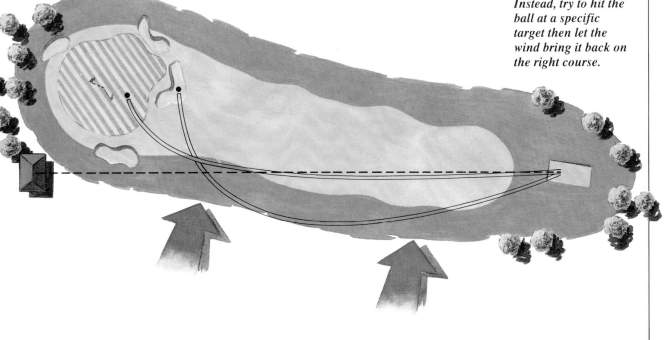

Stand firm

In winter there are no longer firm, dry fairways to add an extra 20 yards to our tee shots; as the courses take on their winter garb, many of those drive and short iron par 4s take two 'Sunday best' woods to reach the greens.

However, winter golf can be enjoyable, provided that you adopt the right attitude to playing in less than perfect conditions. Winter golf, in my opinion, should be fun, although many clubs run winter league and knockout tournaments and competitions can be just as keenly contested in winter as they are in summer.

Nevertheless, I have always looked to the winter months as a time to work on my game and try to correct some of the numerous faults that have plagued me throughout the summer.

Just as the rules of the game, with one or two exceptions, do not differentiate between summer and winter, neither does the golf swing; the same fundamentals are just as relevant in the depths of winter as they are at the height of summer. However, there are one or two aspects of the winter game worth considering which may not only add to your enjoyment, but could also lead to someone else paying for the drinks in the bar after your round.

Playing golf in the winter can often be frustrating; one minute you are scrambling to get your waterproofs on before you get soaked, and next the sun comes out and the temperature suddenly goes up ten degrees. There are numerous other inconveniences attached to playing in winter, but most keen golfers, myself included, are usually prepared to put up with them just as long as we can get out on the golf course.

One of the main problems when it comes to winter golf, is the underfoot conditions. If you are fortunate enough to play your golf on a seaside course then you might not notice any great difference.

However, when it comes to parkland layouts, wet and muddy fairways and tees can present several problems.

One of the essential ingredients of a sound swing is a firm foundation. Under normal conditions this does not normally prove to be a problem. However in winter a firm footing is not always guaranteed. One way to help improve your footing is to make sure that the spikes in your golf shoes are free from grass and mud before you play a shot, especially with the driver. This is the club that we usually put the most effort into hitting and the one which also produces the biggest margin of error from a misshit.

It only takes a moment to check your spikes and to remove any grass or mud with a pitch mark repairer or a tee-peg before taking up your stance. In fact it is a

When conditions are wet and muddy, make sure that the spikes in your golf shoes are not clogged up before you play a shot.

FROM TEE TO GREEN

good idea to check the condition of your spikes, and have them replaced if they are worn down. If you do find yourself faced with a particularly muddy teeing area, look around for a better spot from which to play your shot. There is nothing in the rules which says that you must tee your ball up in a direct line between the tee markers.

You cannot tee-up from in front of the markers, but you can play from as far back as two clubs lengths behind them.

You might discover that by adding a couple of yards to the length of the hole you can find a much firmer footing to play from: a trade which, I suspect, will more than compensate for that extra distance.

If the tee is a little bare and muddy you can peg your ball up slightly behind the markers to help find a firmer footing.

Long irons

They say it is an ill-wind that blows nobody any good and in my case a spell of windy weather once produced a definite improvement in my long iron play. Surprisingly this didn't come about simply as the result of having to hit more long iron shots to reach the green when playing into the wind.

I found myself with a few hours free one afternoon and decided to practise rather than play, and after spending half an hour hitting short and medium irons, I reluctantly moved onto my longer clubs. I say 'reluctantly' because, like most weekend golfers, I have trouble getting the long irons airborne. It always seemed that the more I tried to get the ball up, the lower it would fly.

As Ian Woosnam once explained, you should always practise hitting shots into the wind, and although I was facing a pretty stiff breeze I must confess that I had been striking the ball pretty well. However my confidence faded a little as I lined up my first 3 iron shot and, recalling the theory that you should swing every club the same way, I tried desperately to imagine that I was hitting a 7 iron and not a 3 iron.

I was pleasantly surprised with my first effort, for although I would not actually claim that the ball 'soared' into the blue, it did fly higher than normal. Encouraged by this, I continued to hit long irons for the next half hour and by the end of the session, I was actually getting the ball to fly at a reasonable height.

Though I had not changed my swing in any way, I was baffled as to how I had achieved my good results. And it was not until I got back into the clubhouse that I finally unravelled my successful mastery of the long irons.

"It's the wind" explained my local professional, when I asked his view. "You see, what gets the ball airborne is not just the amount of loft on the face of the club,

it also depends to a great extent on the speed at which the ball spins and the effect of the airflow over a dimple pattern on the ball." Not having a degree in aerodynamics, it took me some time to understand what he was saying but once the penny dropped, I realised why I had enjoyed so much success with my long irons.

It seems one of the reasons why the likes of Seve Ballesteros can hit those towering long iron shots is due to a great extent to the clubhead speed they achieve through the shot. This really gets the ball spinning and aerodynamics do the rest. By hitting my long irons into the wind, I was gaining extra spin and lift on the ball which helped get it flying much higher than I could have achieved normally.

Hitting into a stiff breeze, I was gaining extra spin and lift on the ball.

Green guide-lines

When you reach the green, make sure that you repair your pitch mark. It is in wet conditions, when the greens are soft, that most of the damage is done. And unless a pitch mark is repaired almost as soon as it appears, it will never heal properly and the result will be bumpy greens next summer.

It is also important to take care when walking on soft, wet greens, especially in the area immediately around the hole. Remember, there are others playing behind you and golf is difficult enough without having to try and hole putts through a forest of spike marks.

Wet and heavy greens might also require you to make one or two alterations to your usual putting technique. Some golfers prefer to use a heavier putter in the winter, which basically allows you to get a slightly firmer strike without having to alter your normal putting stroke. One very good putter I know moves the ball slightly forward from his normal position at address when playing on wet greens.

He claims this allows him to strike the ball slightly more on the upswing, applying a little top spin to the ball and helping it to roll better. As most of us tend to leave a lot of putts short of the pin on wet and heavy greens, it might be worth experimenting with this idea.

There are also benefits to be gained when putting on wet greens, but you have to keep your eyes open to spot them. When the ball runs across a wet green it leaves a line on the putting surface. As you reach the green look out for paths left by previous putts for they could help you identify the slopes and borrows on the putting surface. And if you are lucky you might even find one on a similar path to your own putt.

(Below) Repair your pitch marks; if they are not repaired quickly, they may never recover properly and the result will be bumpy greens next summer.

Don't be wet!

It is when playing from the fairway in winter that one of the major differences in the rules comes into play. On most golf courses 'Winter Rules' will be in operation and this allows you to clean and place your ball before each shot providing it is on the fairway or the green.

There are two main benefits in being able to clean and replace the ball. In wet and muddy conditions, earth often gathers in the dimples that cover the surface of the ball. If this earth is not removed it can affect both the flight and performance of the ball. Not only will the ball fail to travel as far as it should, it will also fly off line.

At the same time you are cleaning the ball you should also take the opportunity to dry it. In wet conditions, the more water that gets trapped between the face of the club and the ball, the more erratic the result of the shot. Control is more difficult in the wet and it is also hard to get irons airborne. In fact you are likely to get better results playing a fairway wood, rather than a long iron, when conditions are really wet.

Similarly, make sure that the grooves on the face of your clubs are kept free of earth and, if necessary, clean them and dry the clubhead with a bag towel after every shot; preferably while walking down the fairway to avoid holding up other golfers who might be playing behind you.

If the grooves are allowed to fill up with earth, your shots will become erratic. This happens because the grooves are designed to impart spin on the ball and that spin not only helps get the ball up into the air, it also controls its flight.

Playing from the rough in the winter, when the grass is wet, can also provide a few unique problems, not the least of which is catching what the pros call a 'flyer'. This happens when the ball is sitting up in the rough and there appears to be nothing to prevent you cashing in on your good fortune and belting it towards the green.

Winter rules do not allow you to clean and place the ball in the rough. Therefore you have to consider the fact that the ball will be wet, and so will the clubhead as it swings through the wet grass. The combination of the water on both the ball and clubhead means that there will be very little spin applied to the ball and, as a result, it will probably travel considerably further and also lower than normal. This is great if you are striving to hit the ball a long way, but not quite so convenient if you are playing a short iron.

The grooves in your clubs will tend to clog up more often in wet conditions. Try to clean them regularly in order to prevent miss-hits.

When the dimples in a golf ball become clogged with earth, it can affect the flight of the ball. So remember to wipe the ball clean with a dry cloth.

CHAPTER TEN

Practice

Imagine that...

In my case, that old adage which says, that 'practice makes perfect', may not always apply but I can confirm that it helps my performance on the golf course.

I think it was Seve Ballesteros who once said that golf was a game where the better a player became, the more he practised and it is a fact that the pros spend more time practising than they do playing. It is on 'the paddock' as some pros call the practice ground, that skills are first developed and the range of shots that the top players produce, with seemingly apparent ease, are the result of hitting literally thousands of practice balls.

However, the pros do have the incentive to winning large amounts of money to fuel their appetite for practice. On the other hand, we weekend golfers, faced with less glamorous goals to strive for, tend to settle for a half dozen hurried wedge shots, followed by a few smashes with the driver and a couple of practice putts, before dashing to the first tee in the monthly medal. Others, who may have more time at their disposal, can often become either bored or frustrated by practice, depending to a large extent on how well or how badly they are striking the ball.

Years ago, I used to suffer from the latter when it came to practising but then an old club pro, from whom I had been taking a few lessons, suggested a way in which I could make my practice sessions both challenging and enjoyable.

Instead of just aimlessly hitting balls, he asked me to try to picture in my mind, a particular hole that I had either played, or seen on television. For example if I was hitting my 5 or 6 iron he suggested that I imagine I was standing on the 12th tee at Augusta National and to add the additional ingredient of pressure, that I was leading the tournament by one shot in the final round. He asked me to picture the hole in my mind's eye and also the flight of my ball as it carried over the treacherous Rae's Creek and landed close to the flag leaving me a putt for a birdie two.

It took a little time to get myself into the right frame of mind, but once I did, I found that my concentration improved dramatically as did the quality of the shots which I hit. Over the years I have worked out a series of imaginary shots with a range of different clubs and by now, I must have won all four major championships on at least six occasions, not to mention the Ryder Cup twice!

Joking aside, this method of practice has been really helpful over the years and if you are currently struggling on the practice tee, you might benefit from the exercise: after all, there is nothing like winning a major for bolstering confidence!

Make your practice sessions more challenging and enjoyable by imagining a particularly famous hole. In this case I'm thinking of my tee shot for the 12th at Augusta National.

Practise with a purpose

One of the most discouraging aspects of practising, especially if you do not have very much time, is having to pick up your practice balls. And if like me you tend to spray them about a bit, then it seems that you spend at least half your time collecting them.

However, here is a tip that not only eliminates the boredom of picking up all those balls but that can actually help to quickly sharpen up your short game at the same time.

Next time you have an hour to spare on the practice ground, try the following exercise. First hit twenty balls at a pre-determined target. Then, instead of just picking the balls up, use your wedge to chip or pitch those twenty balls as close as you can to your target, which might be a flag or even a brolly stuck in the ground. Repeat the exercise but this time chip the balls with a 9 iron.

If you have enough time, work your way down through the clubs to a 7 iron. You will be amazed how this simple exercise will help you develop a better feel for pitching and chipping.

True, you still have to collect the balls each time, but this can be done quicker when they are grouped closely together.

After hitting practice balls, chip them to one spot. It will do wonders for your short game.

If you have taken the clubs out of the cupboard after a lay-off during the winter months, in my experience it is best to spend some time on the practice ground getting rid of the cobwebs before getting down to the serious stuff.

The problems I suffer when getting 'back into the swing' every year are too numerous to mention and usually take the rest of the season to sort out. However, I have found a quick and simple method to check whether or not I am hitting the ball off the centre of the clubface. And all it takes to establish this important fact is a strip of white adhesive tape.

Before you hit any practice shots, simply stick a strip of the tape on the face of your club, lining up the edge of the tape with the bottom edge of the club. Then hit about a dozen balls before checking the clubface. The ball will have left an impression on the tape, showing exactly where you have been making contact. Too far right, and you've been striking the ball too far towards the toe of the club. Too far left and you are hitting towards the heel.

If you find that the mark is smack in the centre of the tape every time, then find someone to play for money, as soon as possible!

Making your mark

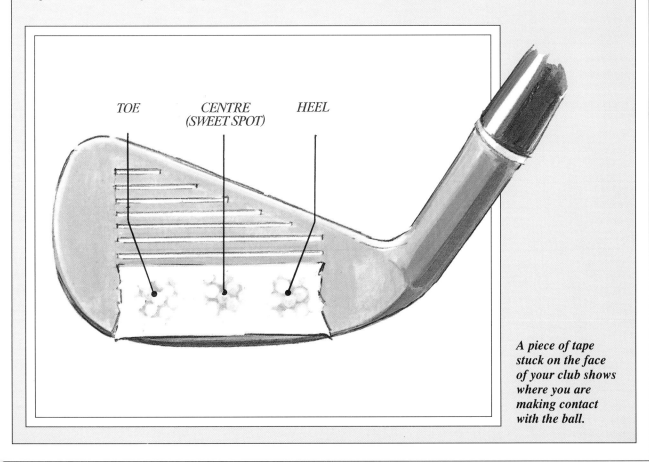

TOE   CENTRE (SWEET SPOT)   HEEL

A piece of tape stuck on the face of your club shows where you are making contact with the ball.

Keep it simple

I was once invited to play in a local Pro Am tournament and prior to teeing off spent a few minutes by the practice green trying to find a miracle cure for my ailing short game.

I had been suffering from one of those frustrating periods that most golfers experience, enjoying a purple patch with my driver, and my iron shots, although not quite arrow straight, were also in pretty good shape.

My frustration stemmed from an indifferent short game, especially from just off the putting surface. And my all-too-rare purple patch from the tee and the fairway was going to waste as I consistently failed to get up and down in two from around the green.

On this particular day, I had dropped a few balls a couple of yards from the edge of the practice green and then started to lob shots towards a hole some 15 to 20 feet away. As usual, it all seemed too easy when I was practising; a long, slow swing and the ball would lob gently into the air, land softly on the green and run to within a few feet of the hole. However on the golf course it was a different matter. The long slow swing then became a short, quick jab and I inevitably found myself trying, and failing, to hole a series of twenty footers for pars.

Looking round the practice green, I noticed one of the other competitors chipping from around the same distance but what held my attention was seeing him hole two out of six shots that he played and leaving the other four balls almost stone dead. I also noticed that he was using a technique totally different from mine.

Instead of lobbing the ball high in the air with a loose, wristy hand action, he was using what appeared to be an extension of a putting stroke. And although the club being used looked to be a wedge, because

there was no wrist action in the swing, the ball stayed low and ran most of the way to the hole along the ground.

The swing looked to be controlled by the shoulders rather than the hands, which seemed to remain subdued throughout the swing. However, the hands were well forward at address and the backswing looked to be instigated by the left arm and shoulder pushing the club back from the ball. The clubhead stayed fairly low to the ground throughout the backswing and the hands and left arm remained well ahead of the ball through impact.

Desperate times call for desperate measures, so I spent the last few minutes before my tee trying to copy this chipping technique. I took half a dozen shots to get the hang of playing this type of shot but once I firmed-up my wrists and kept the club on a low swing path, I was encouraged by how easy this shot was to play and how accurate it was for judging both line and distance.

Sad to say, that day saw the end of my purple patch with the driver and my irons also went off the boil. But as so often happens in golf, my short game turned out to be deadly!

To get the ball close to the hole keep the hands ahead of the ball throughout the swing. Also keep the wrists firm and the clubhead low to the ground.

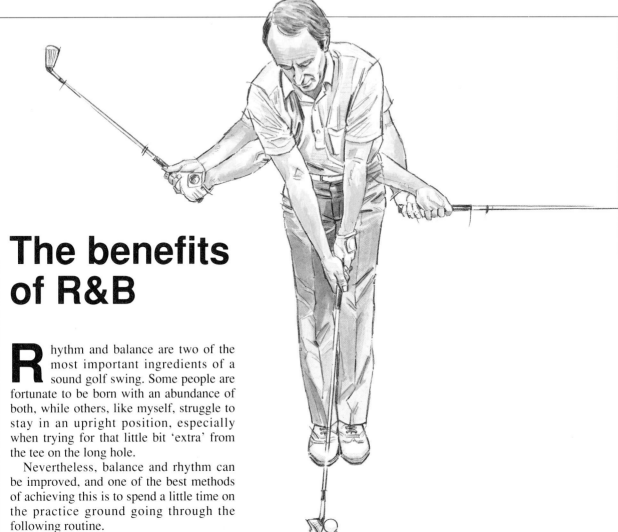

The benefits of R&B

Rhythm and balance are two of the most important ingredients of a sound golf swing. Some people are fortunate to be born with an abundance of both, while others, like myself, struggle to stay in an upright position, especially when trying for that little bit 'extra' from the tee on the long hole.

Nevertheless, balance and rhythm can be improved, and one of the best methods of achieving this is to spend a little time on the practice ground going through the following routine.

Using a 7 iron, stand with your feet close together and start to swing the club back and forth to approximately waist level. At first you might sway about a bit but once you get the hang of it, you will soon develop a reasonably smooth rhythm and better sense of balance.

The next step is to start hitting balls from this same position and that's where the fun usually begins. This is because any attempt to snatch the club away too quickly in the backswing can easily land you on your backside; while a hurried jab at the ball in the downswing can send you lurching off in the opposite direction.

Remember, you are not trying to hit the ball any great distance. In fact at the start you might find it difficult enough just making contact! But once you build up a sense of rhythm and balance, you can start to extend the length of your swing, still keeping your feet together, until you reach the point when you are able to make almost a full swing. You'll be surprised by just how far the ball will fly even with your feet still close together. The benefits from this type of practice session are invaluable for not only does it clearly demonstrate the value of balance and rhythm in the swing, it also helps to emphasize the role of the hands in timing the shot.

To help develop your sense of rhythm and balance, use a 7 iron and swing at first without a ball.

Tune up your timing

T iming is of paramount importance when it comes to making a good swing. Certainly, other factors such as grip, posture, ball position, etc all play a major role, but if your timing is off, then everything else seems to follow suit.

When our timing does become unsynchronized, we tend to speed up rather than slow down, as frustration takes over and we start to hit at the ball, rather than swinging the club through it.

There is one way that I have discovered to slow down your swing and that is to practise swinging something heavy such as two, or even three, clubs at the same time. But recently I was introduced to another method of slowing down my swing and that was to practise with a heavy duty broom. You simply grip the handle the same way as you would a golf club and make a full swing.

The weight of the broom makes it virtually impossible to swing fast and at the same time, it makes you much more aware of things like shoulder turn and weight transfer. The follow-through is another area where swinging the broom can help. Provided that you can muster up the strength to swing the broom from a reasonable top of the backswing position, the momentum which it builds up in the downswing will virtually pull you through to a full, follow-through position.

The broom handle method slows down the swing.

CHAPTER ELEVEN

Left handers

Tips from John Nolan, professional at
Cavendish GC, England.

Left in line

Posture is just as important for left-handed players as it is for right-handers. When setting up, ensure that everything is parallel to the target line — shoulders, hips, knees, feet and eyes. Adopt a relaxed posture and let the arms hang freely to allow them to swing unimpaired.

The left shoulder is a big problem for left-handers. Because it is the stronger side, there is a tendency for the left shoulder to take over the swing. Usually it moves out and opens up the shoulders so that the body is aiming right of the target, causing the player to pull across the ball.

One key to keeping the shoulders swinging on line is to tuck in the left elbow at address. This keeps the left shoulder below the right as it should be and lets the shoulders turn on the proper axis.

Ensure that everything is parallel to the target line — shoulders, hips, knees, feet and eyes.

Left isn't always right

Many left-handed golfers suffer because they let the left side take over in the backswing. They cannot accept the fact that the right side, the weaker side, is the dominating side in the swing for a left-hander.

Two problems can result when a southpaw player lets the left side take over the swing: one, the club is picked up abruptly by the left hand which causes it to start back outside the line

(1)

(2)

(3)

(1), or, two, it is pulled too far inside the line (2) to allow the player to make a proper backswing.

What the left-handed player has to work on is taking the club away from the ball correctly at the beginning of the swing. The most effective way to do this is to push the club back from the ball in a one-piece motion at the beginning of the backswing (3). To facilitate this action, the leftie has to hand over control to the right side.

By pushing the club back with the right hand and arm, the left-hander will

guarantee that the club starts on the proper path. Then it is just a matter of allowing the body to turn naturally to complete the backswing.

Work on controlling the swing with the right side and you will develop a swing that starts back naturally from the ball: your swing will also have a better chance of staying on line.

(1) Pulling back inside the line.
(2) Standing back outside the line.
(3) Pushing back a one-piece motion.

Positional play

Finding the correct ball position is just as important for the left hander as it is for the right hander. Often an inch or two can mean the difference between hitting the putting surface or being in the bunker.

Set-up for most shots with the ball just inside your right foot. This ensures that your right arm and club are in a straight line down to the ball. By adopting this address position, you can guarantee that your hands are slightly ahead of the ball, which is fundamental when striking the ball.

Setting up with the right arm and club in line has another benefit: it means that the right shoulder is higher than the left shoulder at address, the way it should be for southpaws. This set-up also promotes a smooth, one-piece take-away from the ball.

So work on your set-up and ball position; it may mean you will be reaching for a putter more often than a sand wedge.

For most shots it is best to set up with the ball just inside the right foot, ensuring that the right arm and club are in a straight line down to the ball.

Southpaw striker

If you talk to left-handed golfers, most feel aggrieved at the lack of teaching manuals for them. But is this really a problem? Many left-handers find it better to learn from a right-handed professional.

The golf swing is the same no matter whether you're right-handed or left-handed. When a right hander demonstrates the grip and set-up to left-handed pupils they see a mirror image of their own grip. Right-handers should benefit in this way when being taught by left-handed professionals.

As in the case of a right-handed player, left handers should ensure that the club sits in the fingers of both hands and not in the palms. You should be able to see two or three knuckles on the right hand. The Vs created by the thumb and forefinger of each hand should point to the left shoulder. Don't make the mistake of holding the club too tightly in the left hand as this will take the feel out of the shot.

The golf swing is the same for both left- and right-handed players.

Acknowledgements

We would like to thank Brian Waites, professional at Hollinwell GC, Notts, England for the tips on pages 84 and 86. We would also like to thank John Nolan of Cavendish GC, Derbyshire, England for the tips on pages 156, 157, 158 and 159.